In Man We Trust

IN
MAN
WE
TRUST

The Neglected Side of Biblical Faith

Walter Brueggemann

John Knox Press
ATLANTA

Portions of Chapter II appeared originally in "The Trusted Creature," *Catholic Biblical Quarterly,* Vol. XXXI (1969), pp. 484–498. Used by permission. Portions of Chapter IV appeared originally in "Israel's Moment of Freedom," *The Bible Today,* Vol. XLII (April 1969), pp. 2917–2925. Used by permission.

Library of Congress Cataloging in Publication Data

Brueggemann, Walter.
  In man we trust.

  Includes bibliographical references.
  1. Wisdom literature—Criticism, interpretation, etc. 2. Jews—History—To 586 B.C. 3. Theology—20th century. I. Title.
PS1455.B78 1973   261.8   72–1761
ISBN 0-8042-0198-6

First Printing

For Jim and John

> choosing their way to gladness
> and sorrow—and ours
> *Prov. 10:1.*

Foreword

It's a difficult time for the faith of the church, because we have the feeling that the old formulations won't quite do, but we are reluctant to give them up. When we ease off for a moment, we revert easily and comfortably to those formulations. It is an equally tricky time in Old Testament scholarship because the scholarly consensus of the last decade is now showing cracks and seams and threatening to collapse. It is a wrenching time to try to be human—our problems seem so unmanageable and our resources appear to be less than equal to the problems. We are tempted to fatigue and cynicism, or if more sensitive, just plain despair.

The following discussion tries to explore elements in the Old Testament which perhaps make contact with our needs and questioning in the midst of all the trickiness. In some ways the following discussion is radical—radical from the perspective of our usual Bible interpretation with its commitment to a theology of sin and salvation. It is radical from the spiritual heritage of the author, which is not very different from the heritage of middle America, a mixture of evangelical pietism and neoorthodoxy, an uncomfortable mixture but we have taken deeply from both sources. What follows here is a suggestion about biblical interpretation which may correct some of our overzealous commitment to these two sources. Considering our profound commitment to those options, the suggestion is for a fairly radical break in our way of relating to biblical faith.

This book suggests a fresh hearing of the Gospel in the traditions of the Old Testament. Israel's affirmation of faith is many-sided. One of the dimensions which has been largely neglected in our use of Scripture are those traditions which affirm the world, celebrate culture, and affirm human responsibility and capability. Such affirmations from the Bible sound strange to our ears, but they are no less scriptural and no less Gospel. This stress and the literature which express it are, of course, not all of Scripture but they are an important element. I have argued here that for our moment in cultural history, these elements in Scripture provide our best opportunity to make contact between biblical faith and the culture in which we do our "faithing."

To that end I have tried to penetrate the teaching and intention of the wisdom traditions, especially as they are embodied in the book of Proverbs. The study of the wisdom traditions of the Old Testament is only beginning and there are many unresolved questions. But we know enough to suggest some directions for theological reflection. On the basis of the wisdom traditions I have tried to pay attention to the cultural world in which they had meaning, for that world was not unlike our own.

This book, for better or worse, has been my own struggle to come to other alternatives in appropriating biblical faith. It has not been so much a writing as a probing to deal with uneasiness about where we have been. My debts are great. Among Old Testament scholars, the work of Professor Gerhard von Rad looms very large. But most of all it has been a shared pilgrimage with my colleagues, students, and a host of patient and alert lay people, who have urged and driven me to ask such questions and have been open and receptive along the way. The result is not a disciplined, measured interpretation of biblical texts, as I should like it to be, but a moving in and out between where we have to live and with what we have to believe. It is not the best way to write, but at least it is writing the way we have to live.

The discussion begins with a statement of the fresh resources and disturbing questions which are involved in the current recovery of the wisdom traditions of the Old Testament. Chapters II–IV seek to explore one era in Israel's history, the United Monarchy, when the issues between faith and culture were unsettled and unsettling, and several options presented themselves. Out of this exploration I have suggested in Chapter V that our own contemporary theological probing is a troubled struggle with the same issues the United Monarchy faced: the issues of power, freedom and responsibility, and the possibility of maturity which can come only with some kind of authentic faith. Finally, because this is a book which has been nurtured in the church and is addressed to it, I have suggested in Chapter VI what these new trends in biblical interpretation might mean for our common ministry. In some ways I have been led to a radical suggestion which is not radical in the sense of discontinuity, only radical in that it means a recovery of something we always knew but have preferred to forget.

The book is dedicated to my sons Jim and John. In their own ways, in their early years, they are struggling with the same questions and with the neoorthodox evangelical pietism of their parents. Visits to the tombs of Europe's great men and confrontation with the great cathedral art have evoked hard questions of faith, culture, and maturity. For the moment they are a happy quiver full (Ps. 127:4–5).

Even when I am finished, it strikes me that this is an awkward way to express biblical faith, but in our moment, biblical faith, where it is powerful and relevant, will be awkward.

WALTER BRUEGGEMANN
St. Louis, Missouri

Contents

I.
Religious Despisers of Culture[1]

Something important is afoot in Old Testament scholarship which goes under the general heading of "wisdom." A group of texts and a field of investigation which have been long neglected suddenly claim our attention. There are a host of unanswered questions related to the study of wisdom materials. The older notion of wisdom was confined to Proverbs, Job, Ecclesiastes, and in the larger Canon Ben Sira and Wisdom of Solomon, plus a few Psalms: 16, 37, 49, 73. Now that definition will not hold because scholars are suggesting that forms and substance of wisdom thought are found in many other places in the Old Testament. This larger notion of the wisdom literature has given dramatic impetus to study but has also made precise delineation very difficult. In spite of these problems, the new interest in the general subject is important because it opens to us *a dimension of Israel's faith, thought, and life* which we have not fully understood or appreciated.

This study is quite aware of the difficult and unanswered critical questions, but enough is clear that we may address the central question of what this dimension of Israel's heritage means for us who seek to be persons of faith and at the same time persons in culture. In what follows, we will consider especially the fresh resources and insights offered by the wisdom materials for coping with the problem of being simultaneously persons of faith and persons in culture.

It is important that until very recently the wisdom materials have been given little attention by scholars. We have assumed that they really didn't belong in Scripture; indeed, they have hardly been regarded as authentically Israelite. This rejection of wisdom as a legitimate part of Scripture is not simply an accident nor is it a bias on the part of the scholarly community. Rather, it reflects a stance which has characterized the Christian community generally, and especially the Protestant tradition. In what follows, I argue that the recovery of wisdom materials as a legitimate, perhaps even central feature of Scripture, constitutes a considerable threat to the theological establishment that dominates much of Protestantism, but also offers it new opportunities.[2]

The major features of wisdom theology stand in direct contradiction to the central tenets of much church faith. The issue may be put in terms of the title of this chapter. The wise in Israel characteristically appreciate life, love life, value it, and enjoy it. They appropriate the best learning, newest knowledge, and most ingenious cultural achievements. By and large, Protestantism, for a variety of reasons, has been a culture-fearing, culture-negating tradition. This does not properly belong to Reformation traditions and certainly not at all to the Swiss reformers who were much influenced by the humanism dominant in their time. But for whatever reasons, the latter-day children of the Reformation have tended to regard cultural phenomena as a threat to the faith.

In the nineteenth century, Schleiermacher faced a difficult task: the enlightened community who loved life and delighted in its cultural achievements had written off the Christian faith as irrelevant to its cultural context. In our day, the situation in the church is a curious reversal of that. The church is filled with people who value the faith, and for the sake of what they think is the faith they despise culture and all that it means. The revival of wisdom studies raises serious questions and no doubt creates new anxieties for the characteristic obscurantism of much Protestantism.

Several contrasts can be noted between what has become characteristically Protestant in our time and what is characteristic of this fresh dimension of Israel's faith—that which we are calling wisdom. (We refer here to the mood of Protestantism because we know that best. Presumably some of the same criticisms can be made of the regnant Catholic mood.)

First, wisdom believes that the goal and meaning of human existence is *life*. Roland Murphy has asserted that the "kerygma" of the book of Proverbs is "life."[3] The sentences and instructions of Proverbs are designed to provide guidance on how to create and maintain life in all its fullness. The evidence for the validity of such a statement is copious:

> He who heeds instruction is on the path to *life*,
>   but he who rejects reproof goes astray. (Prov. 10:17)

> The fear of the LORD prolongs *life*,
>> but the years of the wicked will be short. (v. 27)

This "kerygma" obviously is not the invention of any theologizing of the material; it belongs characteristically to such observations and instructions. In very old non-biblical materials such as "The Instruction of Amen-em-opet," the same yearning for and promise of life is apparent:

> Give thy ears, hear what is said,
> Give thy heart to understand them
> . . . .
> If thou spendest thy time while this is in thy heart,
> Thou wilt find it a success;
> Thou wilt find my words a treasury of life,
> And thy body will prosper upon earth.[4]

Of course, it is important to understand what is meant by "life." It does not mean, as often it does in our day, longevity or mere survival. Rather, it refers to all the assets—emotional, physical, psychical, social, spiritual—which permit joy and security and wholeness. It includes "all these things" (Matt. 6:33) which let a person reach his full capacity. Obviously such a yearning for and promise of life is never entertained for a person in isolation. In Israel and the ancient world generally, the hope for life intimately links a person to his fellows, so that the promise of life applies to the community in which he lives:

> When it goes well with the righteous, the city rejoices;
>> and when the wicked perish there are shouts of gladness.
> By the blessing of the upright a city is exalted,
>> but it is overthrown by the mouth of the wicked.
>> > > (Prov. 11:10–11)

The self-vindication of Job (31:1–34) is also a statement that his responsible actions have been concerned with the well-being of the entire community. Thus, the *life* which wisdom sees as the goal and meaning of human existence is the well-being of the community and each of its members, i.e., *shalom*.

Moreover, "peace" for the whole community is intensely here and now. There is no "reward in heaven." There is no deferred dividend. Rather, the life which results from wise action emerges together with the wise action:

Hope deferred makes the heart sick,
but a desire fulfilled is a tree of life.

(Prov. 13:12)

Misfortune pursues sinners,
but prosperity regards the righteous. (13:21)

The righteous has enough to satisfy his appetite,
but the belly of the wicked suffers want. (13:25)

Wisdom does not ask a person or the community to wait. Well-being comes in the process of choosing wisely. Thus, wisdom affirms that the goal of responsible living is intrinsic in the very process itself. Being able to live *shalom* is both the wise action and the happy consequence. It is this responsible aliveness that wisdom prizes, the experience of "abundance" (John 10:10) for person and for community.

This view is not generally held among the religious despisers of culture who comprise the center opinion in the church. The goal and meaning of human life is generally regarded as *extrinsic* to the historical process. It is not to be discerned in the process itself but it is something imposed upon the process, or it is something deferred until the end of life.

The guide for responsible life in characteristic Protestantism often is not that which makes for life, yet the point of reference lies outside the experience of life, in the will of God or the law of God. This frequently has placed believers in a curious position of embracing the laws and rules and norms held to be "the will of God," but at the same time they are against the embrace of life as we have characterized it. The result has been an ethic which sometimes has seemed to be against life rather than for it, and the construction of a god who is against life in all its fullness.

Examples of this are all about us. They include the church's fear of and hostility to the theatre and art culture in general. The church has also manifested an unwillingness to take seriously the messages of contemporary youth cultures, even when those messages are concerned with human freedom and social justice. The curious consequence is too often a rejection of the "abundant life" about which we make profession.

To make the goal of life extrinsic to the process, the church ethos has often spoken in terms of another world. Much of the hymnody of the church has ended in the affirmation that "heaven is our home." Thus, waiting—postponing—has become a primary virtue held open, especially for deprived groups such as the Black community in America which has been invited to accept suppression because in a heavenly realm "things will be different." It hardly needs to be reported that a goal extrinsic to the process itself has led to a devaluing of the historical process, a disengagement from it, a cynicism about it, a rejection of it. The consequence of such an opinion has been a church which has cared less about *life for the community* than another goal which is yet to appear. From time to time, the church has not really cared if "a city is exalted" or if "it is overthrown" (Prov. 11:11). This anticipation of an extrinsic goal which has dominated the church has also played a great role in Western culture. It is one of the sources of uninvolvement and social indifference which now plagues affluent America: we don't really care, and often our theology has taught us that we don't need to because meaning is elsewhere.

Wisdom represents a protest against such a deferred goal. It is pragmatic and impatient. It affirms that life's values are embraced or rejected here and now—any other approach which lets us off the hook is quite irrelevant. Any talk of the *will of God* which doesn't lead to life for the community here and now is idolatry. Anything which creates life for the community, no matter what its source, is the will of God.

Second, wisdom affirms that the *authority* for life is to be discerned in our common experience. What is right and good is not identified by answers in the back of the book, but only by patient, careful discernment of what we ought to be doing to be *us*. Wisdom takes a very utilitarian view of what we ought to do:

> Liberalness is good and ought to be practiced because it makes a man wealthy (Prov. 11:25).
>
> Graciousness is commended because the gracious person is honored (11:16).
>
> Diligence is endorsed because it brings a person effectiveness and influence (12:24).
>
> Discipline for children is recommended because it results in a certain kind of child (13:24).

> Tranquillity, as we are so slow to learn, gives a man bodily health (14:30).

Now this may be common sense, but if these values are not weighed carefully, one might well draw contrary conclusions:

> Liberalness may lead to exploitation.
> Graciousness could lead to being taken advantage of.
> Diligence can just make a man weary, but not influential.
> Discipline of children might simply result in a tense family situation.
> Tranquillity may lead one to get left behind.

Thus, the first group of maxims, and many others which might be cited, are not mere common sense. They are a bold affirmation about life, a confession of faith that rejects the contrary view as being false and therefore illegitimate. Wisdom is a patient sorting out of what brings life and what does not.

The voice which lays these affirmations upon the listener with some authority is not appealing to any government, human or divine. There is no *office* which gives sanctions to these teachings. There is only the authenticity of the statement itself, only an invitation, only a "try it and see."[5] The validity of the teaching rests upon the fact that life really happens that way. There is no other court of appeal. The teachings simply assert that life is like that! Authority is based only on seeing it as it is.

Again, this view is not generally held among the religious despisers of culture who comprise the center opinion in the church. There is a general mistrust of human opinion, a predisposition to devalue our capacity to discern what is real about life. Because we minimize our human ability to discern this, in the place of considering human observation we are inclined to speak about the "Lordship of God" over life. It is likely that the virtues of liberalness, graciousness, diligence, discipline, and tranquillity are appreciated and celebrated in the context of such an appeal to authority.

One of the reasons for this is they are considered sanctioned by divine government: these are virtues because God has declared it so and has revealed his will to certain authoritative persons. Obviously, revelation is a difficult business. Norms and controls, though tricky, are needed to supervise revelation. Such an appeal to a norm or authority tends to give some person, or office, or institution a monopoly on a correct understanding of right and wrong while the others are left waiting for a benevolent disclosure of what must be done. A current case in point is the vacillation of the Roman Catholic Church on the birth control issue. The authorities deliberate while the faithful (some of them) wait for an announcement. This notion of moral monopoly is found not only in Roman Catholicism, but in every part of the church which appeals to established authority for guidance. Such "structural" authority has become increasingly disfunctional in our current context.

By contrast, the wisdom teachers do not claim for themselves or grant to anyone else a monopoly on wisdom (cf. the protest of Job 12:2–3). God's will isn't all that esoteric. He does not grudgingly disclose his will only on occasion for some to see. His will is writ large for any who will trouble to see (Deut. 30:11–14). This is not the same as letting every man have his own way. Rather, it is to insist that in the process of social experience itself those who value life can read the demands made upon them. The moral action in each case is that which makes for life.

It is for this reason that wisdom is international in its outlook. A sense of moral responsibility is not peculiarly Israelite, does not belong to covenant, is not characterized as covenant law. Rather, it is there for every discerning person who will choose life. Our moral failure is not resistance to an authoritative teacher, person, or institution. Rather, it is our dullness, our wanting others to make our decisions, our settling for old rules or easy guides, our assumption that life will come in some other way than by our willingness to choose it and pay up:

> He who ignores instruction despises himself,
> but he who heeds admonition gains understanding.
>
> (Prov. 15:32)

Nothing here about rejecting God's sovereignty, only despising one's self—rejecting one's own ability to discern life, forfeiting one's opportunity for life-giving and life-receiving, and settling for the ignoble states of dullness, foolishness, and stupidity!

Wisdom lets nobody off the hook by reference to God. Nor does it give anybody special prerogatives by virtue of exceptional authority. My impression is that the church, by contrast, has fostered a kind of piety which "places it all in God's hands" and an understanding of prayer which looks blindly to God for guidance and answers. Too often this is a not very subtle form of copping out so that we don't have to make our own choices and exercise responsibility.

Third, wisdom affirms that man has primary responsibility for his destiny. Repeatedly, the wisdom teachers observed that the choices a man makes and the loyalties he honors call down upon him a happy or an unhappy lot:

> Death and life are in the power of the tongue. (Prov. 18:21)

> He who pursues righteousness and kindness
>   will find life and honor. (21:21)

> A righteous man falls seven times, and rises again;
>   but the wicked are overthrown by calamity. (24:16)

The clear affirmation of wisdom is that human choices fix human destiny. This teaching has often been presented in caricature as a hard, impersonal, retribution system, as in Job. No doubt the seeds of retribution theology are here, but to dismiss wisdom teaching in that way is really to miss the point. The wisdom teachers are not so doctrinaire as to care primarily about a theory of retribution.

They are more likely to call upon persons to assume responsibility for their lives and the life of their community. Wisdom is not a warning that "you'd better watch out, 'cause Santa Claus is coming to town" and "he knows if you've been good or bad." The mood of wisdom is not a desperate warning, instead it is an affirmative summons to man to recognize the tremendous opportunities which lie before him if only he will seize them.

Wisdom affirms first of all that man is able to *choose wisely* and *decide responsibly.* He doesn't have to be wicked or foolish. He really has an option. Wisdom teaching makes no sense if it is assumed that man's decision-making machinery is hopelessly warped or crippled. The wisdom teachers believe that in every situation the discerning man can make a wise or a foolish choice. He may act in ways which draw nearer either to death or to life. There is no situation in which he can be indifferent about his choice, or in which the choice is hidden if he is discerning, or in which he is unable to choose. Wisdom is addressed to man seen in his strength; when he has the courage to function responsibly.

Wisdom affirms secondly that man must choose in every situation. His being human means that he is continually set in situations where he must exercise his humanness through responsible decision-making. The wise man is the one who knows "the buck stops here." There is no way out. There is no answer in the back of the book. There is no authority to which he can appeal. He is now man come of age in a world from which the gods have fled: it is his world. He is charged with overseeing it, and whatever future he would have he must choose for himself and his community. No man is caught in a place in which he may not choose and no one is guaranteed a place which he cannot forfeit by his choices:

> A slave who deals wisely will rule over a son who acts shamefully.
> (Prov. 17:2)

Wisdom believes and has seen great reversals and inversions in life. But these processes have human explanations. They are not written in the stars nor willed by the gods. They are ordered by men who act responsibly or renege. It is a thoroughly human task but not one that goes beyond human resources.

However, this view is not generally held among the religious despisers of culture who comprise the center opinion in the church. Our theology in a variety of ways has led us to take a dim view of ourselves and our fellows. The theology that has emerged from the Paul-Augustine-Luther line has spoken primarily of fallen man, one who has had all his powers and abilities crippled so that he is unable to act in his humanness.

This theology affirms that man is unable to choose. Even if he tries to choose, because of his fallen condition he will without fail choose death rather than life. Indeed, he has no real option. Such a theology of man has been reinforced by traditional psychological theories. But much recent psychology has moved in other directions which bear upon our theologizing task. And for that task, Israel's wisdom teachers are pertinent.

The question posed by wisdom to our conventional theology concerns the role of man in determining the destiny of his community. In our conventional theology, and perhaps most clearly expressed in prayer practice, we leave these choices in the hands of God. We pray for peace. We pray for well-being. We pray for responsible government. This is not the case with wisdom. No doubt Israel's wisdom teachers believe in prayer, but clearly they do not employ prayer as a way of passing along our responsibilities to God. These tasks belong to us—peace, justice, well-being. What we are called to achieve cannot be avoided by turning it over to God. When these problems are solved they will be solved by human choices requiring courage and insight. God will not do our work for us. A human future is possible only when we exercise human responsibility.

Wisdom is not unaware of the limits to human insight and capability, as von Rad and Zimmerli have shown.[6] But within these limits human persons are held under great expectations. Humanness is seen in wisdom teaching to be an exalted role from which much is expected. By contrast, in the thought of the church our humanness is more often an excuse than an opportunity: "After all, I'm only human." In wisdom such an attitude is not thought to be worthy of our humanness for it is a foolish choice which leads to death. It is an abdication which rejects responsibility and expects someone else (perhaps God) to do our living for us.

The issue is put most sharply when we look at the way the church has treated people in its work of preaching, teaching, and counseling. With few exceptions we have not thought man could be trusted.[7] We have thought he needs to be frightened off, scolded, contained, reprimanded. He needs to have his decisions made for him, for he is both unwilling and unable to make responsible decisions for himself. Over a period of time it would seem that this theology has created a community of men (better, sheep) who function best in such a context. But we need to ask whether this is man as he is intended and could be, or if we have castrated him to fit the scheme. Wisdom teaching protests against our violation of the mystery and glory of man. He has been trusted by God and our thinking about him should mirror that trust.

Fourth, wisdom believes that man is meant for an orderly role in an orderly cosmos. His rightful destiny is to discern that order and find his responsible share in it. The order of life is characterized in wisdom in many ways. In Egypt it is Ma'at. In Israel it may be called integrity (Prov. 10:9), instruction (10:17), fear of the Lord (10:27), righteousness (11:6), prudence (12:23), good sense (13:15), and it is referred to by many other terms.

Whatever it is called, it is a remarkable confession of faith in the benevolence of life, in the staying power of our world, in the possibility of wholeness, in the health of right relations in right community, in the security every man may have without seizing what is his neighbor's. Moreover, in Israel's faith this orderliness to which man may conform himself is not an accident, but is the knowing arrangement of a generous, benevolent god. Life is meant to be stable and orderly; God has willed it so.

The maintenance of the order he wills is related to the quality of our choices; among them are honesty, justice, integrity, loyalty, faithfulness, and insight. The universe is not designed to be a place of upheaval, conflict, and friction (Isa. 45:18). It is not assumed that one must find his well-being at the expense of another, but that each person has a legitimate share which he may embrace without wanting more. (Note the connection between coveting [Luke 12:13–21] and anxiety [Luke 12:22–31].)

This view is not generally held among the religious despisers of culture who comprise the center opinion of the church. The whole scholarly enterprise which understands Scripture in terms of the "mighty deeds of God" structures Scripture around the decisive *intrusions* of God into the historical process. Thus, the Exodus event is a *disruption* of the Egyptian situation. The return from exile is a *disruption* of the Babylonian arrangement. Jesus of Nazareth is a *disruption* of the Roman-Jewish settlement. Surely this is faithful to the intention of these texts. Theologically we have valued the *discontinuities* and ignored the continuity of abiding order in culture and the texts which affirm them.

Conversely, because of our inability to live only by intrusions, we construct order and communities of our own. The order and stabilities we often value and wish to identify with God's purposes are characteristically *partial communities* which are appropriately called "ghet-

tos" whether economic, social, racial, political, or whatever. While
they may appear to be orderly and stable, because they are partial they
are in fact unstable and disorderly. They cannot lead to life but are
rather a comfortable way of choosing death. To choose such a "separate peace"[8] is a form of folly against which wisdom speaks. Wisdom
rejects both notions on the basis that: (1) life is found in just order and
not simply in disruptions; (2) partial communities are not viable
communities for the pursuit of life.

We are victims of a curious combination of assumptions. We
reject order theologically and yet socially we are engaged in construct-
ing little orders which are inevitably phony. Wisdom would offer
another hope, namely, a notion of order which permits dynamic
interaction and embraces the whole human community. Again, wisdom is not just common sense but a bold affirmation of what could
really make for healthy life by those granted the burden and possibility of history.

Fifth, wisdom is the celebration of man as the king of creation.
Man's capability and responsibility have already been mentioned, the
next step is to say that man's capabilities and responsibilities have to
do with his relation to his natural and social environment. He is not
ordained to be man in a vacuum, but in relation to his world. He is
a part of this creation as he relates to the Creator. But he is a special
creature: he is the trusted creature, the ordained creature, the en-
dowed creature, the enthroned creature. He is a part of creation but
he is not permitted to disappear into the landscape.[9]

Wisdom makes an assumption about man, namely, that he is
empowered over the cosmos. It also makes an assumption about the
creation wherein man has his function. Creation is viewed as a good
place to live, a healthy environment, intended by God to be enjoyed.
It is a place of orderliness and security, a friendly place, a healthy
environment, one which opens to man its fruits and its secrets if he
will have it so. Wisdom affirms that the essential mark of a man is his
coming to terms with the opportunities and responsibilities of his
social and natural world. For this reason Zimmerli and many scholars
following him have affirmed the close connection between wisdom
and creation: "Wisdom thinks resolutely within the framework of a
theology of creation."[10]

The wisdom teachers reflected on the splendor, order, beauty, and goodness of creation. They reflected especially on the crucial, strategic role of the man-woman relationship as one responsible for the maintenance and celebration of the life-giving reliability of creation.

Again, this view is not generally held among the religious despisers of culture who comprise the center opinion in the church. The characteristic expression of Christian faith is "Christ died for our sins." Such a view of the role of Jesus Christ in our history necessarily assumes an emphasis upon the character of man as sinner, so that Jesus Christ meets the central need of man by rescuing man from the bondage where he is trapped. This single emphasis has provided a clue for the salvation-history approach to the Bible which concentrates on the traps in which man finds himself and the corresponding actions by which God delivers him. Scripture has been interpreted primarily around the theme of redemption which tends to stress the gracious, powerful role of God and the despair and helplessness of man. The upshot is a self-understanding based on persons of low self-esteem, ill-equipped for the decisions required by our power and knowledge.

As a result, the countertheme of creation has been generally neglected, for it posed a threat to the centrality and decisiveness of Jesus as he has been conventionally interpreted. Our usual theology, which stresses Christ's *saviorhood,* requires an orientation which takes a dim view of the world, a low view of man, and a rejection of all his cultural achievements. It seems to be assumed that only the centrality of Christ is secure.

Out of wisdom quite another approach to the Gospel is possible. Jesus Christ may be presented not simply as savior from sin, but also as fulfillment of the summons to Adam in Genesis. In Christ the purpose of God for "mature sonship"[11] has now come to fruition. Our faith in Christ as Lord confesses him not only as true God whom we serve but as true man in whose manhood we may now share. His true manhood, as ours, consists in his ability to order his social and natural environment for the sake of healthy human community. This way of understanding him, which is in keeping with the creation faith of the wisdom traditions, in no way detracts from his decisive role in our faith; instead it provides a way by which we may celebrate and contribute to the cultural achievements of the human community.

Now, if we look at these five affirmations which belong to the wisdom tradition, several things become clear.

1. Man is a trusted, valued creature in God's assessment, and he may therefore be trusted and valued by us.

a) The goal and meaning of human existence is healthy human community which God values and for which he has ordered his cosmos. Such a view rejects the notion that the goal of life is extrinsic to the process and is to be found in another world. The latter view, which has great influence in the church today, tends to devalue and depreciate the significance of the human community and its well-being.

b) The norm for instruction and guidance is in the careful discernment of what squares with life and is found to be authentic and effective for human life. The well-being of human community is the measure of responsible living. This is the norm for the faith the wise affirm. Such a view rejects the popular notion that moral norms are invested in some special authority, as though they have been given from some higher source. Wisdom values human enterprises as an adequate norm in themselves.

c) Man's destiny is given into his own hands. He is trusted and empowered by God to choose his future. This is contrary to the common notion of leaving things in the hands of God, which often becomes justification for an act of irresponsibility. The world is put together with high expectations for man.

d) Life's meaning is a dynamic, responsible order, in which every man has opportunity for humanness. This is against the common view that God is only a disrupter. Wisdom values the continuities of the human community when they are responsible.

e) Man's vocation is establishing a meaningful relation with his social and natural environment. It is a good and healthy relation. This is against the common view that man's proper stance is against the world and his hope rests in being taken out of it. Wisdom affirms the goodness of human life.

2. We have given considerable attention to the normal views in the church. I hope these are fair and are not a caricature. Here I

simply suggest that these generally held views serve to enhance the special claims of the community of faith at the expense of the human community, i.e., they have resulted in imperialism.

a) The notion that the goal of life is beyond the historical process in another existence has tended to give to this particular community control over passage. This community has claimed for itself the right to determine who shares in the goal and who is excluded. (Consider for example the influence Matt. 16:19 has exercised in the history of the church.) Against this, wisdom affirms that the goal of life is there for every man who will choose it.

b) The church has affirmed that the norm for moral teaching and guidance is the will of God which it often claims to profess. The practical consequence is that the church has claimed the right and responsibility of giving moral guidance. Whoever wants to know must inquire of the church. Against this, wisdom affirms that the norm for action is to be discerned in the very process of living. This information is withheld from no one nor is it entrusted to any particular agency. It is there for those who will observe.

c) The notion that human destiny must be left in God's hands calls attention to the life and practice of the church, particularly its sacramental system, as the way God has granted whereby human destiny is assured. Wisdom affirms that our destiny is not linked to any historical institution, not even the church, but is left open for man to choose and determine.

d) The affirmation that God is discerned only in the disruptions which come upon us has tended to devalue human life, history, and culture. It has stressed instead the uniqueness of the church which is gathered around the memory of decisive disruptions. Against this, wisdom indicates that meaning is also found in other historical forms which stress solidarity and continuity. Meaning is found in order, and we need not seek it only in the disruptions over which the church presides and to which she gives meaningful interpretation.

e) The church has claimed that man stands in need of redemption and asserts its own decisive function in the redemptive process. The counterview of wisdom is that man is invited to choose his full humanity as a creature of God, and obviously there is no monopoly on that process.

Such a way of setting the faith of the wise men against the narrower claims characteristic of the church calls into question the monopoly often assigned the church and the authoritarian stance which seeks to protect that monopoly. In facing the recovery of the wisdom traditions as an important dimension of Scripture it will be useful to recognize some of the aspects of threat which will be felt by the church and her clergy. Very often our understanding of ministry has been primarily informed by the assumed monopoly and its authoritarian implications. Often our understanding of mission of the church toward the world has also been informed by this view. It is readily apparent that the protests of wisdom against this view pose a threat to every form of parochialism and every pretension to authoritarianism.

Wisdom does not render the church irrelevant nor does it abolish the ordained ministry or the urgency of mission. It does raise urgent questions about the assumptions of some *forms* and *goals* the ministry and mission of the church have when these forms and goals are not related to a concern for responsible human community.

The problem with the religious despiser of culture is that we have too often been engaged only in a religious vocation of despising. We have not "loved our brother" (1 John 4:20) in the sense of affirming his humanness. We have for psychological, cultural, and political, as well as theological reasons, not trusted men, not honored them, not believed in them. As a result, we have, over a period of time, created a humanity which really cannot be trusted. We have formed a community of the immature who need some authoritarian pattern to give meaning to existence. But the Gospel, discerned by the wise and embodied in Jesus of Nazareth, says that man can be trusted, honored, and believed in. It's risky business, but God took such a risk.

II.
The Trusted Creature
The Shape of Davidic Reality

The next three chapters explore the revolutionary changes, both cultural and theological, which came upon Israel during the brief period of the United Monarchy. It is in this period that Israel experienced the risk God took in trusting his people, and we explore that period in the context of the questions we have raised in the previous chapter. If the issue is set as a crisis in the relation between faith and culture, then this period can be seen as a shift in which persons of faith began to give positive valuation to culture. They stopped being despisers of culture and became its devotees, a change which turned out to be a mixed blessing.

These chapters are not concerned specifically with wisdom. But they are based on the assumption that it was the mood and faith of the wisdom traditions which created a context for the cultural and theological revolutions which occurred. Thus our central theme is maturity in faith, but this maturity comes to its clearest expression in the wisdom traditions.

In the present chapter the distinctive and remarkable role of David is considered, as he embodies the new mood of culture and theology. In Chapter III the various traditional, literary, intellectual efforts to express the new mood are considered. In Chapter IV I have attempted in summary fashion to trace the revolutions from Saul to Solomon and to consider the blessings and curses which came upon Israel as the revolution moved to its extreme expression under Solomon.

David as Problematic Innovator

It is the understatement of Israel's history to say that David is an innovation in the self-understanding of the community of faith. Israel had never known anything like him before and was not to see such again, in the period before the Christian era. Indeed, David is historically and theologically something of a misfit in terms of his antecedents. He cannot be easily assimilated into any of the already existing forms and structures. The David presence poses the difficult question of what the faith is to do with a radical innovation for which there is no precedent. It is clear that in the Old Testament traditions he is something of a spectacle and at the same time something of an embarrassment.

David marks an ending in terms of the classical formulations of salvation history as it is recounted in the liturgies. In Psalms 105, 106, 136, he is not mentioned. In Psalm 78, a Psalm focused upon the claims of the Davidic dynasty, his achievement is the point of the liturgy but also the end of the recital. There is nothing after David. In Nehemiah 9, the period after him is mentioned, but in terms of the Moses tradition with no attention given to the Davidic presence. In Acts 7, the most complete presentation in the New Testament, David and Solomon are mentioned, but that is all. All of these recitals, either by stopping just before or just after David, recognize that he represents a crucial turn in biblical history. A new form of history has begun which is not properly "salvation-history." This is part of the innovation which the Prince from Bethlehem represents. The old categories cannot contain him.

Closely related to the new form of history is the new form of historiography. Von Rad has shown clearly that the style and presuppositions of the Succession Narrative (2 Sam. 9–20; 1 Kings 1–2) are quite in contrast to the pre-Davidic materials.[1] In the earlier ones the center of the material is the cultic experience and the central actor is God. In the David materials, especially the Succession Narrative, the materials have moved from sacral matters and cult to the affairs of politics and history. Now men make the major decisions and live with the consequences of their choices. This is not writing without faith, for God is still present and decisive, but the style and assumptions are now radically secularized. Israel's history since David has become more properly human history in the modern sense of the word. This is historical narrative which in form is not for liturgical recital and in scope is not in the context or horizons of the credo. It is historical writing which has broken away from the liturgical, cultic environment in which Israel's earlier traditions were kept alive. By its very form this historian shows that history now is presented as the task and burden of human agents.

If the recital ends with David and the form of history writing is now altered, then the question of institutional continuity is raised in acute form. The ordering of Israel's life before David is amphictyonic, or federational. This indeed is what the tensions of First Samuel are all about, with Samuel holding to that order and Saul trying to find room in that context to be king.[2] But with David, the center of power and authority, of responsibility and prerogative is shifted. To be sure, the tradition has now been formulated to suggest continuity between David and the old order. David himself is at pains to claim continuity, as in the movement of the ark, the sign of the amphictyony, and perhaps in the marriage to Saul's daughter. But clearly the dominant move is in another direction—one becomes immediately aware that the discontinuity is much greater than the tradition means to suggest.[3]

There is now present in Israel one who cannot be understood in terms of the older patterns and models. The monarchy as embodied in David represents a radical innovation which will not be subsumed under the already existing structures. Though he courts the amphictyony, he will not be contained by it or reduced to it. The conservatives in Samuel and First Kings were right in discerning that the foundations of corporate life were being radically changed.

The shift is noticed not only in relation to the amphictyony from which he moved away, but also in relation to the non-Israelite life toward which he gravitated. The innovation of David is an experience of positive appreciation of syncretism.[4] In the tenth century, under the leadership of David, Israel ceased to be a minority community in the hill country and emerged into the larger world of ancient Near Eastern power and prosperity. With the new material blessings of such a transition there were also new ideological and theological resources at hand, either to reformulate the faith or compromise it, depending on one's perspective. It is clear that royal theology, alien to the older Israelite community, became a live option for Israel under David.

Probably one source of the new theological horizons was the Canaanite establishment of Jebus (Jerusalem) which David took over with the conquest of his new capital city. There is now no doubt that royal ideology was appropriated which gave important support to the new ambitious regime. In addition to Canaanite influences from Jebus, it is clear that the borrowings from Egypt were large and influential. It just was not to be the same Israel ever again. David drove Israel to radical pluralism. To be sure, this comes to fuller expression in Solomon, but there can be no doubt that it is the genius and boldness of David which sets the pattern for Israel who now must live among the nations as she never had to do before. The shock of this innovation can hardly be overestimated. It demanded of Israel a quite new self-understanding.

This innovation in the life of Israel was of such a radical nature that the tradition builders were left with a perplexity about what it meant. This is evidenced by the diverse, even contradictory pictures we are given of David. Israel in her reflection seems unable to make up her mind in any clear way about who David is or what he is like. He is pictured as the not very impressive youngest son of a shepherd (1 Sam. 16:6–13).[5] He is viewed as the wonder boy admired by the crowds (1 Sam. 17:6–9); as a hard-nosed schemer who will have his way (2 Sam. 11); as the efficient planner and politician who with some struggle maintains order in his own house. He is also pictured as the man of faith (2 Sam. 12:13; 15:25–26; 16:11–12), a theological innovator who functions effectively in terms of tradition and liturgy (2 Sam. 6:12–19; 12:16–17). Added to these is the role attributed to him in the royal Psalms by which he is regarded as the "rainmaker" and the hope of Israel. The tradition obviously knows it is in the presence of greatness, but is not sure how to order its description of that greatness. It is clear that a simple historical or biographical presentation mixed with romanticism will not do, for this greatness is linked in all parts of the biblical tradition with the meaning of history itself.

In his radical innovation David also created a theological and cultural context in which wisdom emerged as a live option in Israel. Although wisdom literature in the Bible is often dated much later than David, and in the tradition intrudes with Solomon, it seems legitimate to suggest that David made this intrusion possible.[6]

David is unique in his openness to the culture about him, his movement away from the amphictyony, and his ability to enter history pragmatically. In David more than in any other person in Israel's history the way is opened for a view of life which takes insight from whatever source is available and accepts learning from any authority. He accepts responsibility when it is thrust upon him and does not ask about the gods and the drama of heaven. David views life as essentially a human enterprise. Wisdom in the Davidic narrative is discerned in the Absalom incident with the woman from Tekoa (2 Sam. 14:1-20), in the counsel of Ahithophel (2 Sam. 17), and perhaps in the shrewdness of Joab (e.g., 2 Sam. 19:5-7). David prepares the way for a new perspective toward human history, responsibility, caring, deciding, and the human use of power.

David and His Theological Revolution

Perhaps now we can press behind these general observations to ask what really was happening in Israel in the time of David. First of all, we should note the difficulty of separating the judgments of his contemporaries and the traditionists from the historical fact. We can hardly ask about David himself, but only about theological disclosures permitted Israel in this time of David. Thus the tenth century witnesses not only a historical and personal innovation, but a theological revolution of the first rank, made possible by David.

Second, because we are interested in the theological consequences rather than the biography of David, we shall need to be on guard against every temptation to psychologize. There is little warrant to try to guess what David felt and thought, for we have data only to discuss what Israel discerned and affirmed in the midst of this event.

When we ask about the theological revolution in the tenth century we come to our central hypothesis: David is pictured as a responsible, free man, and the reason for this is he believed he had been fully trusted by God, or at least so his theologians have presented him. Now this is a remarkable and decisive turn in Israel's faith. It is the affirmation that "man" is not under law.[7] He is trusted to live as he wills to live and is given great responsibilities which he cannot ignore. This theology is an affirmation about God. It affirms that he is not simply the giver of Torah or doer of spectacular saving deeds in history, though he does such deeds.

Now this radical statement is affirmed: what God does first and best and most is to *trust his men with their moment in history.* He trusts them, sets them free from the need to please by law, cult, or piety. He trusts his men not to bring death but to do what must be done for the sake of his whole community. Israel discerned that David knew this and understood his life as an expression of that understanding. Perhaps the rest of Israel's history is an attempt to recover from the dazzling, staggering affirmation of who man is ordained to be by God. No wonder it caused a theological revolution which we say reached its fulfillment in that other "David" on Easter morning. Now we turn to the texts to explore this remarkable innovation.

1. The first text to consider is 1 Samuel 21:1-6, the narrative in which David flees for his life, comes hungry to the shrine at Nob and is given bread to eat by the priest, Ahimelech. The crisis in the narrative occurs because there is no bread available for the hungry refugee except the holy bread which is consecrated to the god. The priest is careful to maintain the rules of piety and questions David carefully on the qualifications of his men for the bread. He insists that his men, though on a profane journey, are qualified for eating holy bread. It is not clear how this argument is pursued, for the text is far from clear.

a) David apparently appeals to the old sacral rules of holy war in which "holy" refers not to what happens at the shrine but to the keeping of old tabus related to war. In this case it means those who go to war keep away from women for a period of three days, not unlike the preparation for the covenant meeting of Sinai (Exod. 19:10–16). David seems to argue that his men are really "holy" and so are qualified to eat.

b) Since this flight through Nob is a flight for his life, without any announced destination or preparation reported, the veracity of David's statement is presented, perhaps deliberately, with considerable ambiguity. David's men are not "holy" as indicated, but David simply asserts against the facts that they are. This judgment is supported by the assertion of 1 Samuel 22:22, that David has done something to bring on the death of the men. Most likely the risk in which he involves his men is related to his revolution against the established order. In such a revolution, one cannot sort out historical and theological factors, but the revolution clearly was a life-and-death matter.

Since we are not interested in the history of the story, nor the motives of David in any psychological sense, we can move on to the point that concerns us, namely the juxtaposition of *ḥol* and *qodeš,* "profane" and "holy." David rejects the conventional notions of what is holy which are upheld by the priest. It may be that he argues that the scope of the holy is very broad so that even the profane journey may be taken as holy. Thus he breaks the notion of holy away from the shrine and moves it out into the normal affairs of men. Or perhaps he regards the notion of holy as secondary and will risk a violation of old tabus for the sake of his well-being and that of his men.

Either way David is not bound by the normal notion of what is *qodeš*. He subordinates that conventional notion to the problem at hand, namely his safe getaway. What remains is the primacy of his welfare and that of his men. If *qodeš* still functions as a meaningful term, it now refers to the well-being of his party on the way to royal power. Against the narrower notions of holy which had been held, this is a revolutionary affirmation made good by his readiness to act upon it. He risks a new idea of what is holy. The way in which Jesus makes reference to this story in Mark 2:23–28, confirms the point our discussion makes. Jesus utilizes the text to overturn conventional notions of what is sacred. David is his bold predecessor in the same effort.

2. In a second text, 2 Samuel 12:16–23, David faces the death of his child. The child is his illegitimate son by Bathsheba and, as tradition gives it, has been cursed by God. The child lingers for seven days, and during that time David mourns and fasts and is not responsive to pleas that he act differently. The story turns in vs. 20 when David discovers that the child is dead. Immediately he ends his mourning and weeping and begins to live again, to eat and drink and be himself. In the child's sickness he gives himself to the sick child. When the child dies, David gives up the child and goes on with the process of living.

The story makes clear that this behavior also is against the tabus of the time. In David's desolation his circle of advisers want to tone down his mourning but he resists them. His mourning must be total and complete. Conversely, his advisers think he should mourn death. For the conventional religionists of his time, it is the moment of death and not sickness which calls for abasement and all the ritual acts. But David sees it differently. David believes that the moment while life lingers is the time for prayer and perhaps appeasement, but the moment of death means facing up to the new situation and living accordingly. In that moment he must turn loose his son and go on with the business of living. He is not impressed with the conventional notion of ritual uncleanness at the point of death, any more than he is impressed with it when he is hungry in the previous episode.

David's reaction to the death of his child and thus to the reality of all death is not to be viewed as stoic resignation. Rather, it is an affirmation of the theological revolution which David ushers in. David has a fresh view of the meaning of life and death, where his proper hopes and proper fears are to be located. This is more than a violation of common practice. It is an act of profound faith in the face of the most precious tabus of his people. It is not freedom from the moment of death, but from the power of death as it has often been described in myth (e.g., Hos. 13:14).

David had discerned, for whatever reasons, that the issues of his life are not to be found in cringing fear before the powers of death, but in his ability to embrace and abandon, to love and to leave; to take life as it comes, not with indifference but with freedom, not with callousness but with buoyancy. There is no trace of cynicism or despair, only a clear affirmation of what life may mean and what it may not mean, an insight into the way of health and the way of unhealth in his moment of loss: "But now he is dead; why should I fast? Can I bring him back again? I shall go to him, but he will not return to me." (2 Sam. 12:23) Life is like that. All the immobilizing fears of the demons and death and impurity have no place in the horizons of this revolution. Faith must be about life: "Who knows whether the LORD will be gracious to me, that this child may live?" (2 Sam. 12:22)

When life is gone there is no seduction into the notion that faith is about death. It is this buoyancy of being trusted that lets David turn loose, even with joy. For him there is none of the conventional paralysis in the presence of death. He knows death belongs legitimately to history and he has no illusions about affirming some kind of faith which does not know death.

3. A third text, 2 Samuel 23:13–17, is a detached note in the appendix of Second Samuel which seems to correlate historically with 2 Samuel 5:13–25. As it now stands, it serves quite a different purpose, namely to celebrate David's brave lieutenants. The story is anecdotal

in character: David, under seige, longs for water from Bethlehem where the Philistines are encamped. It is an unrealistic yearning and he does not request anyone to get it, but because of their attachment to him, some of his bravest do the daring deed and bring the water to him. In an act of chivalry he pours the water on the ground, refusing to enjoy what his men have gotten him at great risk. He understands intuitively (and that is his greatness) that such a costly commodity is appropriately used only for a sacramental act, i.e., an act which affirms the solidarity of his company. This act he performs by pouring the water on the ground (note that the central motif is paralleled in John 12:1–8).

Obviously too much should not be made of this story, unattached as it is. But it is important that the popular motif is attached to David. The builders of the tradition saw in David a fresh grasp of what life is about. He rejects the opportunity to set himself over his men. (Contrast 2 Sam. 11:14–25.) He resists the temptation to pull rank. His own need or yearning is no cause to forget the humanness he shares with his fellow men. To be sure, this can be explained as shrewdness or humility or whatever, but perhaps it also is a component of the theological revolution the tradition discerned in the moment of David.

Perhaps other stories could be added to these, but the three given above provide us with sufficient material to state that:

> David found his holiness in history and attributed it to no cultic material (1 Sam. 21:1–6).
>
> He knew that death belonged to history, but he was not paralyzed by it (2 Sam. 12:16–23).
>
> He understood his humanness with his fellows and rejected the offer to set himself over those who were with him (2 Sam. 23:13–17).

Interestingly, these stories are not the work of one theologian or author but come from diverse parts of the tradition. For this very reason their common witness may be more important. The picture which emerges is a man who knew himself a free man, responsible and involved, but fully his own. I have no wish to construct an ideal model for humanity but rather to trace the revolution which happened at this point in Israel's history. We are not interested here in David as a hero. Rather the tradition, in reflecting on David, discerns something new about our humanness. It means to affirm what it is possible for every man to be in light of this enigmatic man who so dominated this moment of Israel's life.

Yahweh's Remarkable Commitment

The question we ask about this theological discernment today is: what set David free to be such a man in history? He was not an autonomous man who would go his own way as though he lived in a world where God was dead, for he was an ardent believer (cf. 2 Sam. 12:13; 15:25–26; 16:11–12). He was not a secularist man who believed a man must fashion his own destiny, for he was always mindful of the context of the covenant in which he worked. The construction of the tradition affirms that David's freedom to care and be responsible was not an act of rebellion or unfaith, but *an act of passionate commitment to God.* The radical theological conclusion that humanness means freedom in and for history is grounded in the disclosure of the dynastic oracle of 2 Samuel 7. While the critical questions relating to the chapter are difficult, I assume its core indicates authentic royal theology from the tenth century, probably reflecting liturgical use.

Second Samuel 7 is a remarkable innovation in Israel. It is an oracle which asserts that Yahweh has now made a fresh investment in history of a very peculiar kind. His covenant is not now with a community but more particularly with a royal family. His promise is not now conditional, because there is no provision for nullification. Several features of the chapter may be noted in our effort to understand the boldness of the revolution:

1. The oracle celebrates a remarkable transformation by Yahweh of David's state in life. The change is clearly Yahweh's doing, not David's:

I took you from the pasture to be a prince . . .
I have been with you . . .
I have cut off your enemies before you . . .
I will make for you a great name . . .
I will appoint a place for my people . . .
I will give you rest from your enemies . . .

> I will raise up your son after you . . .
> I will establish his kingdom . . .
>
> (2 Sam. 7:8–12)

We are now too accustomed to these words to grasp their radical character. It's not like Yahweh to sign a blank check, but he has. He has trusted David and turned him loose to make what he can of the great trust vested in him, without reservation.

2. The theological revolution makes a hint at punishment for disobedience, but it is clearly subordinated and stops short of rejection:

> When he commits iniquity, I will chasten him with the rods of men,
> with the stripes of the sons of men. (2 Sam. 7:14)

So far it sounds like the Mosaic covenant with its covenant stipulations and covenant curses. But then this:

> But I will not take my [*hesed*] from him . . . Your house and your
> kingdom shall be made sure for ever before me. (2 Sam. 7:15–16)

"But I will not end my [*hesed*]." These are words never uttered before. Not in all the precariousness of Mesopotamian religion, not in the pettiness of Canaanite religion, not in the stress on obedience in Mosaic faith. Yahweh has promised never to end his commitment. Yahweh has thrown in his lot with this moment and man in history and he has left himself no way out. He has trusted man!

3. The trust is enduring. The adverb "forever" occurs eight times in the unit (vss. 13, 16, 16, 24, 25, 26, 29, 29). To be sure, the adverb refers to a variety of subjects concerning Yahweh, Israel, and David and his family. In the latter portion of the chapter it is the word and name of Yahweh which are said to be "forever." Derived from this is the conviction that the house of David is forever because Yahweh's word guarantees it. It is the irrevocable promise to David which concerns us. Yahweh has made an unprecedented commitment of fidelity to David. This man has now been turned loose by God. He has been trusted.

4. Though highly stylized, the prayer of 2 Samuel 7:18–29 indicates that David—or at least the tradition—understood quite well the radical commitment which had just been made. "This was little to Yahweh." That is, there was nothing in David which warranted this

kind of action. David, or the tradition, has come in this moment (probably a liturgical moment) to a fresh understanding of what it means to be man. God takes the little *(qaton)* and makes him great *(gadhôl)*. The transformation is done without questions asked, without promises made, without guarantees given. It is a bold act of trust on the part of God which turns the new man loose, safe in an uncertain future.

The prayer of David begins in profound gratitude but it moves quickly to another motif. David means to exploit the radical promise, to hold Yahweh to it. He is not prepared to bargain it away or to minimize the implications of the divine commitment. He means to take fully what has been given to him, freedom from a religious system based on law, a myth grounded in appeasement, a morality which is petty, and a piety which is self-effacing. Now the issue is quite turned around. David is free, not without responsibility, not without high expectations laid upon him, but free from the norms and limits which religion had held, including those of the Moses tradition.

David may have exploited and failed and cheated, but his notion of freedom is always in the context of this word which will not be rescinded. He may at times over-live but he will not be tempted to under-live. And that, say his theologians, is what it means to be David. Indeed, that is what it means to be a man. These three memories from David which I have cited were not fabrications nor imaginations, but how David was seen and remembered. It is his theologians who discerned in his life-style something new and different, something about the reality of faith which is best put in terms of freedom and responsibility. They looked at him or remembered him, and it really was that way before their very eyes.

Resources in the Wisdom Traditions

This new presence in Israel evoked a new way of doing theology. I suggest that in the wisdom traditions we may discern the expression of this life-style and bold faith stance. Though wisdom has old non-Israelite antecedents, wisdom in Israel has a peculiar cast, informed especially by the David theology:

1. "The fear of the Lord is the beginning of wisdom." This formula governs the wisdom of Proverbs, even where it is not verbal-

ized. This wisdom is not sheer prudential ethics, pragmatism, or utilitarianism. It has a theological foundation in the lordship of Yahweh, in the confidence in his good purposes and the resultant confidence about the orderliness of life, the reliability of healthy conduct, the integrity of community, and the meaningfulness of human history. This way of expressing one's deepest theological premise does not need to be mouthed continually, but lived as the first principle of faith for the free, responsible man. It affirms that a great deal is permitted and also expected. Man is trusted to affirm what is permitted and what is expected. There are no arguments, debates, or doubts. Rather there is here a bold positivism which lets the free man live rather than reflect, risk rather than ask.

This is the life-style which is most apparent in the life of David. The reason he can take holy bread for profane use is his point of reference in Yahweh who has permitted him all things. David can react as he does to the death of his illegitimate son because he knows the boundaries of Yahweh's commitment to him and he will not seek beyond that boundary for what is not granted to him. In his life with his troops this faith affirmation keeps David realistic about his place in history and the limits which history imposes upon his importance and power.

In other places in the succession document this same faith is apparent. In his flight from Jerusalem he does what he can and then concludes:

> If I find favor in the eyes of the LORD, he will bring me back and let me see both it and his habitation; but if he says, "I have no pleasure in you," behold, here I am, let him do to me what seems good to him. (2 Sam. 15:25–26)

Or in the moment when he is cursed by Shimei, he is tempted to kill his scoffer. But he says to Abishai:

> Behold, my own son seeks my life; how much more now may this Benjaminite! Let him alone, and let him curse; for the LORD has bidden him. It may be that the LORD will look upon my affliction, and that the LORD will repay me with good for this cursing of me today. (2 Sam. 16:11–12)

In both cases David acts the part of a bold man, but knows that some things are not given into his hands. This is more than shrewdness. It is a mature faith which lets him function without needing to function where he cannot. Great freedom and responsibility are combined with ability to leave other matters completely in the hands of Yahweh. Both David and Yahweh have things to do, but they are not the same things. Thus "fear of Yahweh" sets one free both to act and to trust.

David embodies the best of wisdom theology. On the one hand, wisdom saw that man was very much emancipated, that he would have to make his own decisions and was free to do so, that he would have to live with his decisions and accept the results of them, that he could choose his future but then would have to embrace it. The power, ingenuity, and courage of man come to full expression here. But on the other hand, there are limits to human power and freedom and beyond these limits man can go only at great risk. Wisdom has the responsibility to discern in each situation how far man can go and where he must stop short before divine mystery. David is the man who resolves to live up to that very limit, at times honoring it, at times transgressing it. He manifests the courage as well as the awe which is expected of the mature man.

2. W. Zimmerli has explored the centrality of *trust* in wisdom.[8] He suggests that the central question in wisdom is: How do I as a man secure my being? The answer, both powerful and simplistic, is "trust" *(baṭaḥ)*. There are two uses of the word in Proverbs which illuminate our concern. The first of these means that the one who asks the question of destiny relies upon another:

> *Trust* in the LORD with all your heart,
>   and do not rely on your own insight. (Prov. 3:5)

> In the fear of the LORD one has strong *confidence*. (14:26)

> Happy is he who *trusts* in the LORD. (16:20)

> He who *trusts* in the LORD will be enriched. (28:25)

Thus the basis of the healthy life is abandonment of fundamental anxiety to God. David could function in this way because of the promises of 2 Samuel 7. The second use of the term "trust" refers to the result of such abandonment, namely security:

> He who listens to me will dwell *secure* and will be at ease, without dread of evil. (Prov. 1:33)

Then you will walk on your way *securely*
and your foot will not stumble. (3:23)

These uses are closely related to the old covenant traditions which speak the same way (Lev. 26:5; Deut. 12:10; 1 Sam. 12:11).

These are of relevance for our study of David. First, he is the trusting man, counting on the promise, set free from anxiety about his "being," from the law, from cultic practice, from every form of appeasement of the gods. He is free to be his own man, set free by the incredible commitment of Yahweh in 2 Samuel 7. As a result of this new freedom he is the secure man. It is the promise that makes *baṭaḥ* possible. Without it one is engaged in securing his life. This David need not do.

3. The one who fully "trusts" himself to Yahweh is given the gift and task of life in all its richness. The risk of trust and the gift of life are closely related. David is entrusted with life, with the courage to live it, with the responsibility to make it accessible to others. Wisdom is the observation of what makes life possible and what its conditions and its limits are. Wisdom is the affirmation that men are freed to live, freed from the gods or by the gods. Men have only to seize what is offered. This is the picture of a man who is freed for responsibility to create life for himself and for his community.[9]

It seems clear that David embodies this understanding of human existence. He knows that he is meant for life—the abundant life—and he proposes to live it that way. His norm for holy things is that they are given for life (1 Sam. 21:1–7). He knows that his life is intertwined with those of his fellows and he does not want life alone (2 Sam. 23:13–17). He is clear that meaning has to do with life and he has no interest in pursuing the question of meaning beyond life (2 Sam. 12:16–23). His whole existence is the embracing of life. This does not protect him from abuse of life nor transgression of the limits, but quite clearly he is committed to over-living rather than under-living. His violation will not be because of timidity but because of misunderstood freedom (cf. Matt. 25:14–30). Obviously, David represents a new life-style in Israel, a clear knowledge of what it means to be human. David experimented in the style of self-affirmation and boldness and self-possession. This, rooted in the promise which could not be doubted, made it possible for Israel to understand afresh what humanness is about.

From reflection upon David, Israel in the tenth century derived new and profound convictions concerning the meaning of life. David was understood as authentic man and certain generalizations based on him seemed legitimate. Foremost among such reflections is the work of the Yahwist, Israel's most brilliant theologian. In Genesis 2 he asserts a Davidic theology of man. To be sure, the chapter contains all sorts of mythical materials and older traditions, but they have been reshaped in light of David. The J account of Genesis 2, I suggest, is the David career now generalized as the way to be human:

> Man is the goal and purpose of creation. That's what it's all about and for whom it is.
>
> Man is formed of dust, really a nobody, but incredibly trusted by God, i.e., given his own being and turned loose in the Garden of Eden.
>
> He is entrusted with the garden. In Genesis 2:15 there is no other charge given or provision made. The garden has been turned over to man.

In David the theologians saw a different kind of man, one who celebrated life, who knew no limits of a conventional kind, who accepted responsibility, who celebrated freedom, who asserted authority, who risked decisions, and who did not flinch from the ambiguities of his place in life. The liturgic affirmation that stands behind the creation theme in J material is the royal confession of 2 Samuel 7. David has been trusted by Yahweh and that is a remarkable innovation in both the history of religion and the history of man.

I am, of course, aware of the four sin stories (following J) which have been called "the fall." Similarly, Yahwist was aware of the sordidness of the David pattern. In the David narrative, his weeping over the death of Absalom (2 Sam. 18:33) manifests a recognition of the failure of David to live in history on its own terms. Here, in contrast to 2 Samuel 12:16–23, he does not bear his responsibility nor meet the demands of his historical moment. The narrative seems to suggest a deterioration in which David has lost his boldness and stamina. Again, in the Bathsheba-Uriah incident (2 Sam. 11–12),

David shows his inability to live with the givens of history. This data is surely present in the narrative.

In neither Samuel nor Genesis is the intention of the narrative to dwell on the failure. Rather, in both cases the emphasis is upon the buoyancy of God's commitment. They affirm and reaffirm that Yahweh continues to trust and is not prepared to abandon his oath to David. The miracle grows larger, for Yahweh is willing to trust what is not trustworthy. The gospel out of the tenth century is not that David or Adam is trustworthy, but that he has been trusted. Thus the event of David brings to historical realization what the wisdom tradition had hinted at but never witnessed and permits the bold affirmation of the J theologian. If man stands in this relation with Yahweh then it is quite clear that we are concerned with a God quite unlike that about which we have often theologized.

David's Maturity and Ours

If this analysis is in the main correct, several implications of it may be noted:

1. There are important resources in the David traditions for thinking through our notion of man. David's times are not unlike ours: the breakup of the old conventional patterns of security; the end of the old theological assumptions and ecclesiastical institutions as viable forms of life; a new sense of the muscle of man and the potentiality of human ingenuity and self-assertion; a sense of exhilaration and a corresponding sense of confusion. Without need to be simplistic, we may learn something new about what it means to be a man of faith in a world come of age, for in David, Israel came of age.

I am aware that I have presented a one-sided picture of the David notion of man. There is always the tragic dimension, always the helplessness and despair when the promise seems to have failed and the trust given us feels like hatred. The pathos of 2 Samuel 18:1–8 keeps the David tradition in balance. But that dimension has not been a focus in this discussion because it is a subordinate role in the David tradition and because our contemporary cultural crisis requires a new way of putting the question. Moreover, it has been such a central theme in our theologizing about weak, empty man that I believe we must cultivate other areas to recover a balance. In our time our problem is not where we find God in our failure, but how we respond to his trusting us in our strength and success.

2. This dimension of biblical faith may represent an invitation to Judaism. I refer especially to Richard Rubenstein's "core myth." While I have not found the phrase in his writing, Rubenstein has used it in oral presentation to refer to the retribution scheme of good people prospering and evil people suffering, reflected in Deuteronomic and much prophetic thought. Rubenstein believes this has been the dominant pattern of faith in Judaism, and so calls it the "core myth." He concludes that Jews have spent too long trying to please the God of the Deuteronomic-prophetic tradition (who cannot in any case be pleased), so we may and must turn from the God of history, by which he means the god of retribution, back to mother earth.

Perhaps the "core myth" is also a very one-sided reading of the tradition, even if we have done it for so many generations. The David enterprise affirms that in history there is another option, a God who does not need to be pleased but who has trusted us in unflinching, apparently irrevocable ways. The Jewish community is summoned by such a tradition to recover the richness of something long neglected.

3. The Christian tradition faces the problem more ambiguously. On the one hand our celebration of "grace alone" has made it easy to leave everything to God and simply abdicate. It is this "cheap grace" which has encouraged the social irresponsibility so widespread among us. At the same time, we have gone the way of legalism which denies Yahweh's incredible commitment to his people. This is evidenced in our work ethics, our passion for law and order, our social and domestic relations which are based on a demanding and uncompromising works righteousness.

The tradition of David, against both perversions, affirms that we are not invited back to the womb nor are we left alone with our problems. We do not have to do with a God who simply keeps us warm and suckles us without asking any questions, nor with a harsh taskmaster who nags us continually. This strange combination of perversions has produced an American church which is largely irrelevant and immobilized. The resources of the David tradition affirm the centrality of graciousness—a graciousness which cares and asks and expects much from us. The one who trusts has not just trusted us, but has trusted us with his world. So the core myth affirms that we are to "till it and keep it" (Gen. 2:15), i.e., exercise responsible oversight for the world. The Christian community is summoned by such a tradition to recover the richness of something long neglected.

4. This tradition is then important for the ministry of the church, for it affirms that our manhood is not found in under-living, in the "godly, righteous, sober life," but in the human, social, intoxicated life of celebration and responsibility. Our ministry which has often been custodial to confirm people in their status quo is not intended to sustain people and structures in sickness but to call them to health. It is not intended to forgive in under-living, but to call to full living, not to bask in our untrustworthiness but to call us to embrace the trust given us. The image of manhood we have been content to project is something short of the power of the Gospel and—if the David syndrome is valid—something less than the high expectations of the God of our tradition. The humanness entrusted to us is not an excuse for ineptness and cowardice, but a charter for living life to its hilt for the sake of the whole family of God.

5. Finally, the David tradition makes a staggering affirmation in relation to the time of the secular in which we must live. The obvious fact is that the cultures of the future really can't carry many more freeloaders and adolescent adults. They urgently need persons and groups of mature persons, able to risk, decide, and celebrate. The David tradition may provide a set of images which can nurture people to that kind of maturity. This is no panacea. I have not suggested there are no failures or temptations, nor that the demonic is not with us. But after all of that is recognized, the David tradition holds a promise of the kind of persons our future urgently requires.

III.
Theology Fit for a King
Reflections on the Solomonic Crisis

The period of the United Monarchy (1000–921 B.C.) posed for Israel new dilemmas such as it had never experienced before, and offered fresh opportunities for culture and faith such as it had never before imagined possible.[1] What was hinted at in the time of David came to glorious and tragic fruition in the time of Solomon. The newness which was thrust upon Israel touched every dimension of its existence. Economically, control of trade routes gave Israel a kind of influence it had never known (1 Kings 9:26–28; 10:11–12, 26–29). Politically, it was for the first time involved in the internationalism of its world, wrenched violently from the more parochial horizons in which an earlier generation had lived (1 Kings 3:1; 9:24; 10:1–5; 11:1).

Because of the complex nature of the United Monarchy which had absorbed all sorts of people, Israel for the first time struggled with the problem of cultural and religious pluralism in which the conventional answers of the Mosaic tradition no longer could be taken on face value. The prolific marrying of Solomon is of course to be understood politically and therefore theologically (1 Kings 11:1). The narrative is concerned with the facing of various theological options which entered Israel with the coming of foreign princesses. This theological pluralism was supported by the composite structure of the monarchy itself—Solomon was ruler over a variety of peoples with a variety of religious loyalties.

New power, new affluence, new sophistication led Israel to new opportunities for leisure (cf. 1 Kings 4:20–21) and its common partner, reflection. New kinds of questions were being posed which Israel in its earlier, more precarious existence had not had time or inclination to ask. The point of reference for meaning in history was shifting. No longer could the complexities of faith and culture be resolved or accepted in terms of Israel's older institutions. Now the point of reference was the other nations, the more prosperous cultures, the more impressive centers of power and learning. (1 Sam. 8:20 represents a programmatic statement for the mood and values of this culture.)

All of this led to a remarkable literary flowering which has often been noted for its style and eloquence, but has not often been studied for the vigor of the faith and theology that come to expression in it. Von Rad has called this period in Israel her "Enlightenment" and Whybray more recently has spoken of the "new vision of man" which emerged.[2] In terms of our own current situation, we may say that Israel was radically secularized in Solomon's generation. The various literary efforts from the period display attempts to live as men of faith in the midst of secularization. It is this quality that makes these efforts relevant and compelling for our moment of faith.

While we will stress the new illumination that came in this moment, it is important to note a negative problem posed by the Solomonic event. Behind the various efforts toward faith lies the shared recognition that the faith of the tradition, centered in Moses and transmitted as the core of Israel's self-understanding, now appeared to some in Solomonic circles to be irrelevant. To those who had to live in the power and affluence and pluralism of the new age it was surely something of an embarrassment. In any such crisis one can (1) simply repeat the old tradition, which happily these theologians refused to do; (2) abandon the old tradition, which equally happily they refused to do; or (3) work at a radical reformulation of the old tradition with reference to the new situation. It is this last option which these authors and artists attempted with varying degrees of success. However one may judge their success or failure, the effort in itself merits our attention for it is the classic example in Scripture of valuing what has become an embarrassment and trying to reassert its power and compulsion.

On Life and Death

Of the attempts to deal with this crisis, the first we shall consider is the collection of observations in the book of Proverbs. In critical scholarship Proverbs has most usually been regarded as late writing and therefore unimportant. It has been treated as a response to the disappointment and frustration of the post-exilic period. Moreover, it has most often been characterized in pejorative terms—rationalistic, prudential, utilitarian—and so it has not been taken as a positive witness to any sort of mature faith. All of that is now being restudied.

First of all, the late dating is now generally called into question.[3]

The tradition itself (Prov. 10:1; 25:1) claims rootage in the Solomonic period and this corresponds to the narrative evidence that wisdom teachers flourished in the court of Solomon (1 Kings 4:29–34). Thus the earlier dating is gaining increasing ground among scholars. A little thought suggests that the world view of Proverbs is more appropriate to the prosperity of the Solomonic period than to the misery, disillusionment, and poverty of the exile. If Proverbs are dated this early, then clearly they take on a new importance. They are not a peripheral item to be treated with indifference, but now are to be viewed as a vigorous attempt at faith in a time when the old traditions were an embarrassment and the sophisticated successful world of Solomon was impatient with the old formulations.

Set in this context Proverbs may still be described in the same way as before—rationalistic, prudential, utilitarian—but now these are not negative terms. Now we can see that these are theologians trying to hold for faith among the culture despisers who perhaps thought they lived in an age of the Death of God. The narrative of Solomon traces his faith movement from love of Yahweh (1 Kings 3:3) to "love of many foreign women" (1 Kings 11:1). The mood of the monarchy seems to be that we have gotten for ourselves all that we might desire. We owe no one anything; therefore we are free to do exactly what we want with all that we have and all that we can get (cf. 1 Kings 4:20). It is a context of avarice and pride, well documented in the Solomonic narrative and in Proverbs where it is referred to as "folly" (Prov. 15:21; 16:18; 22).

In that situation it would have caused little impact to recite the Commandments, to scold and threaten, to quote the tradition, because the enthusiasts for the new mood felt themselves emancipated from all the old sanctions which hardly seemed to operate any more. It did no good to talk about the great redemptive intrusions of God in the past, because God didn't seem to come that way anymore. Besides, who needed him in the Solomonic situation? It did no good to talk about judgments and commandments because men in this mood are laws to themselves. No doubt some still tried the orthodox approach and no doubt they were deeply disappointed, for in such times conventional religious reminders and reassertions do not get a hearing.

So the wisdom theology, no doubt much of it borrowed from Israel's neighbors and silent on the traditional formulations of the Mosaic faith deposit, is a much more subtle attempt to get through to those who had "escaped the gods," and to so avert the suicidal course of avarice and pride on which Israel was set. There is in this subtle effort no claim to authority, no appeal to tradition, no invocation of any sanctions. There is simply the unencumbered, uncompromising affirmation that life has some givens that cannot be avoided: that certain actions produce certain results; that there is a correlation between our decisions and our destiny; that we have options set before us which give us life or death, prosperity or misery. To think that these givens can be disrupted or altered is "folly" which no thinking person can knowingly choose.

Wisdom teaching is not a very prophetic style because it conceals its sense of urgency. Its profundity is cloaked in seemingly naive understatement but it has a thrust which can hardly be avoided. It is scarcely god-talk, for the gods had been written off in the euphoria of Solomon's time, but it is life-talk and death-talk which can scarcely be disregarded.

The Proverbs continually warn of the danger involved in pride and greed, and this discernment is peculiarly appropriate to what we know of the Solomonic period:

The strong tower of the wicked comes to ruin,
    but the root of the righteous stands firm. (Prov. 12:12)

He who despises the word brings destruction on himself,
    but he who respects the commandment will be rewarded. (13:13)

The LORD tears down the house of the proud,
    but maintains the widows' boundaries. (15:25)

Everyone who is arrogant is an abomination to the LORD;
    be assured, he will not go unpunished. (16:5)

It is an abomination to kings to do evil,
    for the throne is established by righteousness. (16:12)

Perhaps the emancipated mood of the time is addressed in the only way possible. The basic claims of the purposes of Yahweh for the

Davidic house are here enunciated, in a way which could perhaps get a hearing.

There are all kinds of fragmentary matters in Proverbs which cannot be schematized, but two convictions emerge at the center of the proverbial materials: (1) *our decisions matter* in terms of our destiny and we had better heed the choices we make; (2) *there is a givenness about life* with which we cannot tamper despite all our power and influence.[4] The first conviction is present in the tenth-century writings addressed to the selfish indifference and irresponsibility which took life for granted without acknowledging one's accountability for one's own destiny and that of the community. The second is addressed to the arrogance which assumed that enough power and know-how can be assembled to have life on our own terms. This is not so and the wisdom teachers of Proverbs knew it. But Israel under Solomon was so busy that she could not listen in time. It is fundamental to such teaching that wisdom, the antithesis of folly, prolongs life, and that reference to Yahweh is the core of life-giving wisdom (Prov. 10:27; 14:27; 16:22). These texts do not often appeal to Yahweh, and when they do he is not an active agent. But they do assume that those to whom they speak are concerned about life. In the tenth century this means the maintenance of well-being they already possessed. Life is a theme which concerns even the most emancipated secularized man or society. But the wise knew that the things which make for life (e.g., righteousness, Prov. 12:28) are not attractive to those committed to irresponsibility and arrogance. This theology seems to address those bent on folly and its necessary result, death.

On Promises and Betrayals

The second attempt to speak about faith and meaning in the crisis of secularization is found in the Succession Narrative of 2 Sam. 9—20 and 1 Kings 1—2. Two scholarly discussions are pertinent for our understanding of the piece.[5] First, von Rad has shown that this narrative introduces into Israel a new kind of historiography. In contrast to the Pentateuchal stories in which the gods figure prominently and actively, here they are nearly absent. In this narrative, history is essentially a human enterprise. Men are permitted to emerge as complex personages who are studied and appreciated and perhaps even understood. They are presented as persons having the capacity to deal with their moment and who must face their particular crisis. Here more than anywhere in Israel's history men are permitted to be men, free to make choices and live with their consequences. There is no *deus ex machina* here. Men have to find among themselves the resources for coping with their successes and failures.

More recently, Whybray has suggested the connection between the Succession Narrative and wisdom teaching. He has shown, convincingly I think, that the central motifs of the Succession Narrative are quite in keeping with wisdom theology and dependent upon it. He does not call into question the historical reliability of the basic plot of the narrative. There seems no good reason to doubt the movement of the history of the David family. When that is granted it is clear that we do not have in the narrative a report on what happened, but a shrewd and sophisticated reflection on the meaning of the monarchy and the divine promise.

The wisdom themes which we have suggested above are present in a central way, as Whybray has shown. On the one hand, the narrative affirms that if one chooses folly, he will get the consequences of it. This is the meaning of the succession of incidents. David chooses Bathsheba and pays. He "despises the word of the LORD" and gets the result of his action (2 Sam. 12:9; cf. also Prov. 13:13; 19:16). Amnon covets his sister and pays (cf. Prov. 21:26). Absalom chooses rebellion and pays with his life. The story is left open with Solomon. It is not clear what the consequences of his ruthless actions will be and perhaps that is the point of the story, but the hints of death are all apparent there. Solomon will prosper if he is wise and obedient (1 Kings 2:3). But Solomon and his contemporaries scarcely keep the Commandments and so they will not prosper:

> He who oppresses the poor to increase his own wealth,
>   or gives to the rich, will only come to want. (Prov. 22:16)

The Solomonic narrative invites him to "execute justice and righteousness" (1 Kings 10:9), but he has other plans (1 Kings 5:13) which could not possibly lead to prosperity.

On the other hand, like wisdom, the Succession Narrative affirms in a subtle, almost cautious way that the decisions of men take place in the context of a mystery of purpose which cannot be defeated or eliminated. Remarkably, each episode in the narrative ends with the affirmation that in spite of the leaders' unwise choices *there is yet a givenness about the promise* made to the dynasty that has not been voided. All man's "folly" is important and costly but it is not the last word. There is a buoyancy in history and that is the final reality around which the meaning of history clusters.[6]

Perhaps all this boils down to the affirmation that Solomon had better shape up or he will pay like the others have paid before him. But such a bald statement would be a hopeless attempt at communication. Assuming that the story is aimed at the mood embodied in Solomon, or perhaps addressed to the king himself, the point is made persistently but unobtrusively. It is the message that the heir to the throne (presumably Solomon) had better heed the warning of the recent past: those who choose folly cannot avoid the consequences of folly. Those who think they are not accountable, those who think they can do exactly as they please, those who think they are a law unto themselves (as Solomon apparently thought) can learn from the results of earlier choices. There is no opting out. If one does not pay now, he will pay later, as so many of Solomon's kinsmen learned and as the wisdom teachers had unmistakably observed.

Assuming that the narrative addresses the crisis of the tenth century, it affirms that men might get too big for their breeches or their thrones but they are not that big yet. There is a thrust in human affairs which will not be turned aside. In terms of the tradition, the promise of Yahweh will finally be fulfilled. It cannot be voided even by human folly. Thus Solomon (or David, Amnon, and Absalom before him) is not the master of history and the sooner he learns this the better off he will be.

On Freedom and Perversion

The third effort in this crisis, the most complex and probably the most important, is that of the Yahwist.[7] Here we will not deal with the total effort of the Yahwist but only examine prehistory as he formulates it for clues to his handling of the tenth-century crisis. Von Rad has shown that the faithless nations (Gen. 2—11) and faithful

Israel (Gen. 12—50) are set in contrast. This reflects a major concern of the Yahwist, namely, to set Israel's faith in the context of world history, or more precisely, in the internationalism of the world of Solomon. No longer can one presume to be God's special people in a cultural vacuum (which is the tendency of the more parochial traditions of the north), but now if one is to make the claim that Israel is God's special people, he must do so in the presence of non-Israelite peoples. It is to this reformulation that the Yahwist addresses himself. Wolff has refined the work of von Rad by showing that the relation between Israel and the other nations is understood in terms of curses and blessings. Israel is presented as a blessing bearer to the curse-laden nations around her. Thus he reasserts Israel's unique role in history and at the same time gives full recognition to the other nations, as the times surely required.

Now if the theologian can make that presentation stick he has in one bold stroke both preserved the tradition of Israel's election faith and at the same time taken account of the crisis of pluralism. Solomon lived in a mood which seemed to presume upon Israel's special relation to Yahweh; the temple theology seemed to take Yahweh for granted. It assumed that because Jerusalem was his special shrine, surely Israel was safe against all its enemies. This is the popular theology of dynasty which later came back to haunt Isaiah and Jeremiah (cf. Mic. 3:11 and Jer. 8:19).

The Yahwist seeks to retain what is true in that theology by asserting that the blessed people of Solomon do not exist for their own enjoyment but with reference to others. That is in keeping with the assertion we have found in our two other pieces of wisdom literature, i.e., Proverbs and the Succession Narrative. Here also it is affirmed that we have decisions to make and are responsible for them. We are held accountable and are not permitted for a moment to abdicate, yet it is also affirmed here as in other biblical pieces that our decisions take place in a context of hidden purposes which we can neither make nor destroy.

I have attempted to show the relationship between the Succession Narrative and the Yahwist prehistory.[8] I have shown that the stories of the Yahwist, like those of the David family, affirm (1) that each person receives the consequences of his choices, but that (2) there is another dimension, a given which transcends human choices and continually reaffirms man's life and his responsibility. The Yahwist, out of the Davidic experience, has generalized to say that life is like that—that all men are held accountable and that if they choose folly they pay for it. But in spite of our choosing folly there are other purposes alive in our experience which both rescue and crush us from time to time.

I think the connections between the Yahwist and the Succession Narrative are clear. The connections between the Yahwist prehistory and wisdom theology have not been thoroughly studied.[9] While we have no complete study of that connection, a relationship between the two cannot be doubted. In the first of the four "sin stories" of J (Gen. 3) the connections seem clear enough. Blenkinsopp has noted among the major motifs: the danger of the woman who brings death, the link between keeping the commandment and having life, and the image of the tree. Before him, Alonso-Schoekel had noted that "knowing good and evil" was a wisdom theme. To these may be added several other details:

1) The *cunning* of the serpent (Gen. 3:1) plays on a theme common to wisdom.

> The wisdom of a *prudent* man is to discern his way,
>   but the folly of fools is deceiving. (Prov. 14:8)

Thus the delicate distinction between prudence and folly is observed. The serpent gives *folly* for advice but it appears to be *prudence*. The term *'arum* occurs often in Proverbs and relates to "knowing good and evil" (cf. Prov. 1:4; 8:5, 12; 12:23; 13:16; 15:5; 19:25).

2) The serpent in his folly gives false advice about life, for his advice really leads to death (Gen. 3:4).

> He who keeps the commandment keeps his life;
>   he who despises the word will die. (Prov. 19:16)

(Cf. the same motif in Prov. 13:13; 2 Sam. 12:9.)

3) The inordinate desire (coveting) which is expressed in the story is a theme in wisdom.

> The treacherous are taken captive by their lust. (Prov. 11:6)
>
> All day long the wicked covets . . . (21:26)

(Cf. the same term *hamad* in Gen. 3:6.)

4) The curse upon the land for the folly is thorns (Gen. 3:18). This is not an uncommon result of folly.

> The way of a sluggard is overgrown with thorns . . . (Prov. 15:19)

> Thorns and snares are in the way of the perverse . . . (22:5)

> . . . the vineyard of the man without sense; and lo, it was all overgrown with thorns. (24:30–31)

5) The curse upon man is frustrating work (Gen. 3:17).

> The slothful will be put to forced labor. (Prov. 12:24)

("Forced labor" of course became a symbol for the values, mood and policies of the Solomonic regime.)

In the second of these stories (Gen. 4), among the major themes are:

1) The unfortunate results of hot anger and hatred (Gen. 4:5).

> Hatred stirs up strife . . . (Prov. 10:12)

> He who has a hasty temper exalts folly. (14:29)

> A hot-tempered man stirs up strife . . . (15:18)

> Good sense makes a man slow to anger,
> and it is his glory to overlook an offense. (19:11)

2) The foolish are consigned to desolate wanderings (Gen. 4:16).

> The righteous will never be removed,
> but the wicked will not dwell in the land. (Prov. 10:30)

In the third of these stories (Gen. 6—9) there are a variety of motifs which appear to have wisdom connections:

1) In Genesis 6:5 there is mention of the evil imagination of the *heart*. Because the heart is the locus of decision making and because the wise men are concerned with the process of decision making, we will expect to find this motif in wisdom:

> The wise of heart will heed commandments,
> but a prating fool will come to ruin. (Prov. 10:8)

> Deceit is in the heart of those who devise evil,
>   but those who plan good have joy. (12:20)

> Sheol and Abaddon lie open before the LORD,
>   how much more the hearts of men! (15:11)

> The crucible is for silver and the furnace is for gold,
>   and the LORD tries hearts. (17:3)

2) By contrast, Noah is *righteous* (Gen. 7:1) and has *favor in the eyes of Yahweh* (Gen. 6:8). Wisdom celebrated the righteous, the man of integrity, and those who had favor with Yahweh (10:2, 9, 16; 11:4, 19; 12:2, 21, 28; 13:13; 14:27).

3) The major offense of the sons of Noah is that Ham *dishonored his father* (Gen. 9:22). It is not clear how closely this is linked to wisdom, but certainly one delight of a father is a responsible son, which Ham surely was not:

> A wise son makes a glad father,
>   but a foolish man despises his mother. (Prov. 15:20)

> A stupid son is a grief to a father. (17:21)

> The father of the righteous will greatly rejoice;
>   he who begets a wise son will be glad in him. (23:24)

In the fourth story (Gen. 11:1–9) the connections are clearer again:

1) The concern for a *name* to be honored is the point of the episode:

> The memory of the righteous is a blessing,
>   but the name of the wicked will rot. (Prov. 10:7)

2) The major motif relating to wisdom is of course the danger of *arrogance:*

> When pride comes, then comes disgrace. (11:2)

> Before destruction a man's heart is haughty . . . (18:12)

> Haughty eyes and a proud heart,
>   the lamp of the wicked, are sin. (21:4)

3) The *building* is used in wisdom for the symbol of *pride* which must be destroyed:

> The strong tower of the wicked comes to ruin . . . (12:12)
>
> The house of the wicked will be destroyed . . . (14:11)
>
> The LORD tears down the house of the proud . . . (15:25)

4) The use of *"propose"* (Gen. 11:6) is a word often used in wisdom for devious planning which is condemnable:

> A good man obtains favor from the LORD,
>> but a man of *evil devices* he condemns. (Prov. 12:2)
>
> The sacrifice of the wicked is an abomination;
>> how much more when he brings it with *evil intent.* (21:27)
>
> He who plans to do evil
>> will be called a *mischief-maker.*
>
> The devising of folly is sin,
>> and the scoffer is an abomination to men. (Prov. 24:8–9)

Some of these motifs relate the two kinds of material more directly than others, and certainly other examples could be added. But these are sufficient to make the point which concerns us. The movement and basic presuppositions of the prehistory in J writings is informed by wisdom theology, and the point of these stories revolves around a central point: we are held accountable for our decisions and we are free to choose life or death. Certain kinds of irresponsible actions disrupt healthy order and cause undesirable consequences.

These stories present, as does wisdom, an enlightened view of human responsibility and destiny. Wisdom, and these stories, assumes that man knows and that he is free to choose. The stories are a reflection on the choices man characteristically makes and the consequences that characteristically follow such choices. The stories, like the wise men, have confidence in the orderliness and reliability of life. In the midst of this orderliness they also note a strange benevolence which can only be observed but not explained: in the midst of suffering as a consequence for our foolish choices there is still some goodness and sustenance granted to us:

> Many are the plans in the heart of a man,
>> but it is the purpose of the LORD that will be established. (Prov. 19:21)

The J narrative in these early episodes employs mythological themes and images, but the theological presuppositions which determine the movement of the stories is most clearly recognized in wisdom teaching. Again we meet the same two affirmations: (1) our decisions affect our destiny; and (2) all our power and arrogance cannot alter the givens of our existence.

There are complex interrelations between the three literary sources discussed here which are important for understanding any one of the three. We may summarize their apparent patterns of interdependence in this way:

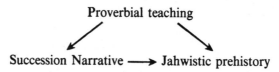

In terms of dealing with the cultural crisis of the Solomonic period, the three sources comprise a remarkable, unique corpus which reflects an amazing literary and theological achievement. To be sure, each of the three has its own characteristic marks, and most notably the Jahwistic materials are cast in a form which has often caused us to miss the primary thrust shared by these three literary pieces. But the three are agreed upon these major points:

> The future is largely determined by our present decisions so we should act responsibly.

> In spite of our best planning there is an inscrutable mystery about our experience which we cannot master or manipulate.

Theology Appropriate for Kings

Each reader will measure the success or failure of these three theological materials in different ways, but at least each of the authors of these materials recognized the crisis with which his contemporary culture had to live. Each knew that one could not hold up the old commandments and ask for obedience, for their compatriots were not prepared for such norms. They knew that they could not bear witness to the old saving deeds, for their fellows felt no need for such "miracles." They knew they could not talk about faith in terms of divine intervention, because these "Renaissance Men" felt such talk was nonsense. So they had the guts to put their theology in fresh ways: we are responsible for the world that emerges from our decisions; we are not free to make the world in the image of our greed and self-centeredness.

It is obvious that these pieces of literature and this way of theologizing have gotten little hearing from those of us who are children of the Reformation. We have done our Scripture studies in terms of man's sin and God's grace, informed primarily by Paul and more particularly his letter to the Romans. Obviously that commitment on our part needs no defense. It is equally obvious that the theology which ought to meet the mood of the Solomonic establishment does not easily square with our core tradition. So perhaps we can look afresh at these alternative ways of formulating faith which are offered to us in Scripture.

1. We have been so afraid of works-righteousness and legalism that we have not developed *a theology of responsibility*.[10] Of course it has been there all along, but we have scarcely noticed it. When the issue is drawn to our attention we have thought it more important, and perhaps rightly, to reaffirm justification by grace. The warnings against folly, the reminders to Solomon, the observations of the Yahwist on the responsibility we have for our decisions, cannot any longer be dodged by our own fear of works-theology.

We are held responsible for our decisions. We do have choices to make which cannot be regarded as trivial. The future is very much the result of the kind of choices we make. No one will make our choices for us. We cannot turn it over to God. We cannot abdicate. Our hesitation in stressing responsibility as a primary theological datum has helped to produce the social indifference and irresponsibility which is all about us in American culture. We, like Solomon, have thought that we were free in our decisions to do what we might like to do and somehow, somewhere, someone else would make it all work. Wisdom theology, reflected in each of these tenth-century efforts, makes it clear that nobody else will make it work out all right. That is up to us. We shall learn from these neglected traditions that a theology of responsibility is not legalism. Because our decisions make the future we are not talking works-righteousness. We are free to speak in different categories because the times demand it.

2. These traditions are reluctant to speak about the intervention of God. He never comes abruptly in Proverbs. Only three times in the Succession Narrative does his purpose make an explicit difference and even in this instance he does not intervene. In the Yahwist writings he seems more directly involved, though that aspect perhaps needs to be reexamined. Alonso-Schoekel has rightly concluded that the "mythical" form of these narratives is incidental, that it is wisdom—not myth—which is decisive for their understanding. In any case, taken together these tenth-century efforts did not make much of the intervention of God. They go in the direction of humanism and are more interested in man's attempts to cope than in the coming of God.

In our tradition, perhaps in contrast to Catholicism, we have been concerned to witness to the Lordship of God over history and have been zealous to claim for him the decisive role in every turn in history. This indeed is the assumption of a salvation-history approach to Scripture. On the other hand, wisdom and the derivative discussions do not celebrate his intervention. They do not credit him with every major turn in history. They believe that human choices play a large if not the decisive role. What then happens to *transcendence?*

Transcendence is often taken to mean the decisive intervention of a personal God, but it can be defined in other ways too. Transcendence is the affirmation that there is a given to the ordering of life which we cannot eliminate. Transcendence is the recognition that there is a mystery to life that is not confined to our ignorance, incompetence, or abdication. There is mystery in our best knowledge, in our greatest skill, and in our most passionate concern. The wisdom teachers and their followers did not care for a "God who acts," but they did know and affirm that life has an order and direction which is larger than human effort and which is not knowable to us. Faith means coming to terms with that direction and order for the sake of those entrusted to us.

It is a staggering task to do theology "fit for a king," but in the tenth century no other kind was worth doing. This is theology for a king who found the old ways irrelevant or easily exploited, so a *theology of responsibility* was more appropriate than talk of obedience, threat, and promise. For this king a *theology of transcendence* could no longer be expressed in terms of a God who acts and intervenes, but in terms of a thrust and order in life which we cannot void. Kings seem not to respond to some faith-affirmations which an earlier generation of peasants has found meaningful. The kings can perhaps still be addressed, although to do so requires fresh options like these with which Israel experimented in the tenth century.

Our task in the church today is to fashion a theology fit for kings: kings of power, affluence, technology, and urbanization. It obviously will not do to repeat for these new kings a theology appropriate to the king of the tenth century, but perhaps there are resources in these traditions we have neglected in our commitment to the formulations and categories of another moment in history. These earlier traditions certainly have the merit of realizing it is a king who must be addressed, and we have not consistently recognized that reality today.

IV.
Tempted to Commodities

In the brief period from Saul to Solomon, Israel's history ran a gamut of emotional states and experienced most of the options open to a historical community. Changes were rapid and radical. In the brief span of three generations the dominant strand in Israel's faith moved from a man in touch with the soil and the people to a tyrant alienated from land and people as well as from the God of whom Israel's tradition speaks.

Too much that is romantic in tone has been written about Saul, but it is surely the case that he was still in touch with the powers that ancient men feared, respected, and sought to manipulate. It was Saul who held to the ancient oaths even if it meant the death of his beloved son, Jonathan (1 Sam. 14:24, 39, 44). It was Saul who in his moment of desperation abandoned the faith of Israel and appealed to the numinous forces which seemed to him to be so powerful (1 Sam. 28:8–19). To be sure, he did on other occasions show another side (1 Sam. 13:8–15; 15:8–9), but compared with either David or Solomon, he is clearly one who has not embraced the radicalness which is stressed in much of biblical faith.

In the categories we are using, Saul stands before the revolution. The vast cultural changes of David and Solomon which required accompanying theological changes had not yet hit Israel in the time of Saul. Thus he shares none of the sense of power, freedom, and responsibility so characteristic of David and Solomon. On the other hand, he is a champion of the old order, with certain appeal to the religious despisers of culture. At the same time and for the same reasons, he is a pitiful figure unable to cope with his historical moment.

David's Israel under Freedom

In the world of Saul, a world of vows to death and appeals to the dead, David appears to be a radical innovator. To be sure, he paid lip service to the older conventions, as when he brought the ark to Jerusalem (2 Sam. 6) and when he showed concern for the heir of Saul (2 Sam. 9). But the whole tenor of his career is that he is not impressed with the old tabus. He is not controlled by old conventions and old opinions.

It is not clear if his new way of operating is to be understood as simply the action of a bold person who exercised his genius without regard to his religious context, or if it is to be read as a conscious effort to make a point. In either case, the tradition clearly shows that David felt himself so trusted by God, so committed to a fresh notion of power, so confident of his own capacities to cope with the situations confronting him, that he acted and lived out of a tremendous sense of his own freedom.

David's freedom is manifested in many ways: his decision to shape his government in the non-Israelite city of Jerusalem; the transfer of military operations from a people's militia to state army; his self-assertion which set a tone for government by royal decision rather than by traditional laws. Indeed, the whole flavor of his person and career was a movement from the amphictyony of the hill country with its parochial, isolated mentality, to the world of commerce and trade. David's reading of the historical moment required a sharp though ambiguous break with the past which had still figured so large in the thinking of Saul.

Indeed, David's times and circumstances called for that kind of radical change in the mood and direction of Israelite leadership. His movement of the ark into his own Canaanite city-state and the liturgical moment in which he receives theological legitimacy (2 Sam. 7) give expression to David's decision to go a new way. The new way was the way of learning, the introduction of wise men into the councils of government (cf. 2 Sam. 16–17). The new way was therefore the way of reflection and asking bold questions which the older generation had never dared to ask nor felt compelled to answer. The new way was one of power—both military and economic—of taking history into one's own hands and giving it shape and direction. There was no need to ask the witches or the medicine men, for now human ends and human policies are taken with great seriousness.

The new way was the way of pluralism: this conglomerate included all kinds of people who shared none of the old Israelite traditions but who paid their taxes, filled their draft quota, and gave allegiance to David and his government. The new way was the way of secularization, the practical orientation of a man concerned with the shaping of history, moving toward a future which can be shaped but not predicted, which can be received but not manipulated. New times required new forms of faith and life and David in his very person embodied the freedom which the times required.

The Loss of Divinity: Secularization

David of course did not measure up completely to the new freedom he claimed for himself. He often overstepped the prudent limits of freedom, but the important point is that he made the attempt and did remarkably well. He forged a quite new life-style which abandoned many of the guides and boundaries which his tradition offered him. In general, he is presented in the tradition as being able to cope with the dilemmas of his fresh freedom in responsible ways. There can be little doubt that the J portions of the creation narrative (Gen. 2) are formed under the influence of the Davidic presence. The model man described there is no doubt a reflection upon David, the freedom granted to him, and the ways in which he used his great freedom.

Thus the freedom which David claimed has caused the tradition to explore in fresh ways the manner in which the royal figure can relate to the things now placed at his disposal. It is first to be discerned that things are just "things"![1] This is a discernment that David apparently made about much of life. He was not impressed by the fears and encumbrances that haunted Saul. He (and the J tradition in the same thought world) understood that God must be taken seriously but that he is not honored or pleased through an undue respect or reverence for things. God is to be worshiped but things have now lost their divinity; therefore, the king has new freedom in disposing of them. This emancipation from the world of spirits and demons in which Saul lived is rightly described as secularization.

The theologians around David had discerned something very delicate about the relation between the king and the world entrusted to him. They had learned that man has a very close kinship with the world around him, that he is made of the same stuff, that connection with things is important to his health, that in a way, man is a brother to the world around him. He belongs to earth (Gen. 3:19).

At the same time they had discerned that this kinship did not

mean equality. Man has been given control over things. Things are at
his disposal. His lordship over his own affairs, i.e., his capacity to
make decisions and live with their consequences, now extends also to
the world of things. He is to "till it and keep it . . . give names" (Gen.
2:15, 20), or as a later reflector on the same data put it, "to have
dominion" (Gen. 1:28). It was a new thing in Israel for someone to
affirm that man is meant to control his natural environment. It was
a thought too bold for Saul's generation to think. Saul characteristically put himself at the disposal of his world without asserting himself
over it. Such a stance surely resulted in his tragic character.

But David's circle of learned men had insight regarding another
extremely important factor, namely, that there is an answerability
concerning man's relation to things. He is free, but he will pay for
irresponsible freedom. He is free to use, but he will suffer if he abuses.
His freedom is in terms of his own intended function in life, to till and
keep, i.e., to care for, to care about, to protect, preserve, and use
wisely. If he does not function in this way, he not only finds himself
cut off from his kinship with his world (Gen. 3:23), but he also learns
that the stuff itself turns sour and unproductive (Gen. 3:18). Man's
self-respect requires facing up to all his freedom. His respect for the
world entrusted to him means to respect the world's rightful use
which is inherent in its very existence.

The freedom of David and the loss of divinity in man's world
were necessary counterparts. They belong together. As the royal man
came to understand his own royal responsibility he came to have a
new freedom with and toward things, a freedom which is not detach-
ment, but in which man's own well-being is very intimately linked to
the well-being of all entrusted to him. David and the theologians who
reflected upon him are indeed the secularizers of Israel and her faith.
Contrasted with Saul, the creation faith of J materials conceives a
quite new position for a man/king in the created world. The importance of David for this new notion of man in and over creation cannot
be overestimated.

Solomon's Israel under Alienation

Sons often seem to be like their fathers, only more so. So it was
with Solomon. He seems to have extended the directions of David's

work until they became something else. What in David had been responsible exploration and celebration, became with Solomon heavy-handed, gross perversion. Perhaps that was already indicated in the manner of his succession to the throne. David had come to power and the people were with him and for him. Solomon had the people against him from the beginning (1 Kings 1—2). David had come at the right moment, when his people were ready for change and experimentation. Solomon came at a time of trouble, division and uneasiness, when his people were weary and disillusioned with the royal experiment.

The cultural crisis which had erupted with David continued with Solomon. The new way set in motion by father was accelerated by son. The new way of learning saw the prudential, calculating manner of wisdom come to increasing influence, an influence which seemed sharp and shrewd and more than a little calloused (1 Kings 3:16–28). The new way of power—military and economic—was continued, but new power was turned against the king's own people so that it became a policy of slave labor. The very citizens he was to govern were made the work force of the regime (1 Kings 5:13). Though there is conflicting evidence (1 Kings 9:22), the rebellion of Jeroboam suggests the mood of the realm. The new way of generous pluralism became a corrupt kind of syncretism (1 Kings 11:1–8) in which no clear moral imperatives were visible and in which no discernible lines of policy set limits to the self-aggrandizement of the regime. The new way was secularization gone crazy—not really secularization, more properly alienation, the loss of every dimension of meaning, mystery, and responsibility. What had been for David an authentic feeling of fellowship (2 Sam. 23:13–17) now became for Solomon big business without any notion of the king belonging to his people or to the world in which they found themselves (1 Kings 4:20–28).

The Loss of Meaning: Profanation

Very often in our discussions of the monarchy, we speak of the "United Monarchy" as though Solomon and David are to be understood as a single historical phenomenon. It is generally understood that David marks a radical shift in the mood and intention of Israel. Here we suggest that an equally radical shift takes place at the death of David and the beginning of Solomon's reign.

We grossly oversimplify if we treat David and Solomon together. Though they dealt with the same cultural crisis and both made radical innovations, the similarity does not carry beyond these general observations. Nowhere is this more obvious than in the theology of "things" which grows out of the work of Solomon. We have said that David took from things the sense of divinity which made him free to handle, control, and manage. Of Solomon we may say that he not only attributed to things no divinity, but he even seems to have robbed things of their worth, as though they had no meaning at all.

No doubt the builders of the Solomon tradition in Scripture are of another texture from that of David. They have neither the literary finesse nor the sense of vitality which is clear in the David tradition, but even after one has allowed for these differences, the quality of the subject comes through unmistakably. David, even when he had secularized life around him, still understood the majesty and excitement of life, the splendor of human relationships, the dramatic quality of a kindly act, the potential for communication in the sharing of a small piece of life, an alertness and sensitivity which keeps life human even in a new age.

By contrast, Solomon understood none of these dimensions of his own life. His giving of justice is the settling of scores (1 Kings 3:16–28), not the healing of life (contrast with 2 Sam. 14:8–11). His military preparations seem related to no cause but simply the weary task of self-enhancement and survival. His building of the temple is a gigantic bureaucratic undertaking quite in contrast to the openness of David's investment of himself in the ritual of his people (2 Sam. 6). His giving of proverbial wisdom is reported as though the main thing is the statistic (1 Kings 4:32). Here is a man and a mood without any human quality, unable to inspire in his people or in the shapers of the tradition any sense of human quality.

How does this kind of man, this kind of regime, this kind of cultural mood feel about things? Things are a bore! They are to be handled—horses and Egypt, chariots and Kue—gold and Ophir—Sheba and spices—but only handled (1 Kings 9:27–28; 10:28). The regime had created a mood in which men only handled things. They did not relate to them. They did not find meaning there. They did not bring them into any contact with their own lives.

"Alienation" is perhaps the right word for it as much as "celebration" is the right word for David. All that David had discerned now seems to be so overstated, such a caricature that nothing of its power remains. Whereas David had learned that things are things and he took delight in them, Solomon came to regard them as *mere* things if he regarded them at all. He did not see in them any of the richness of life to which David was sensitive; they were only objects to barter with to get something else to barter with. Whereas David's attitude toward things had freed him, the new mood of Solomon only emptied him, left him desperately alone, unaddressed by the world around him. David had secularized, Solomon profaned. The world has been robbed of its dimension of mystery and therefore of its meaning.

David had learned that he had an intense relationship with the world, a sense of brotherhood. His kinship with his world is not unlike that of Carl Sandburg who came to know himself in always fresh ways as he communed with his land, especially that of his birth:

> . . . Sandburg excused himself and walked away from the villagers to be alone for a moment in the golden fields nearby. He bent to lift a handful of earth and crumbled it through his fingers. "This is for me holy earth," he said, "and I am grateful to Providence that I got the opportunity to come here."[2]

By contrast, Solomon is protrayed as being out of touch, capable of no relationship of any kind, certainly not with the world of things around him. The differing attitudes are not unlike those of the principals in Steinbeck's *Grapes of Wrath*. It is affirmed that "Pa is the land," and soon after he is ripped out of the land, he dies, for he has lost part of himself. By contrast, in California "everything is owned." Everything is owned and nothing is lived, nothing is loved, nothing is celebrated.

In Solomon's world everything is owned, if owned then sold, if not owned, purchased. Steinbeck insightfully makes "tractor" into a verb. The whole land is "tractored." Solomon, in the biblical tradition, is presented as though he were on a tractor, with no sense of the land he tractors, no feeling for the people whose property he tractors, no awareness of what is happening to himself as he tractors. Solomon does not know that he is of the earth, bound to it, committed to it, responsible for it, answerable for it and to it.

David knew that things were at his disposal. Solomon knew that also, but Solomon forgot as David remembered that there is an answerability to the use of the things entrusted to us. David learned this, frequently the hard way (cf. especially 2 Sam. 12:13–14). The traditionists around him describe it in terms of thorns which come from exploitation (Gen. 3:18) and the restless frustration in our relation to it (Gen. 3:19). But Solomon had bought his way in, seemed answerable to none, had created a religion for himself in which there was no one to whom answer must be made. Things are at the disposal of the king. Solomon's is a strange kingship, for a king must come to terms with his realm. Things make demands upon their rulers. Things are inherently intended for some purpose, and to mock at that fact is to destroy the thing itself, to remove the mystery of life which is there for our celebration, and finally to remove our own names and faces from the Book of Life.

It is not accidental that the J narrator uses banishment as the dominant symbol for the exercise of pride (Gen. 3:24; 4:12; 11:8). Exile, removal from the land of order and meaning, separation from the things which give life depth, is an appropriate symbol for the world of Solomon to which the J theologian addresses himself. Just as "alienation" has become a master term in our time to describe the loss of meaning, so "exile" accurately describes this culture of Solomon which had everything money could buy but found there was no "pearl of great price" available. We are of course familiar with Israel's sixth-century exile, but we have not seen how discerning the tradition is to realize that this exile already begins in the tenth century (1 Kings 11:31–36). Self-seeking power sets Israel toward alienation and exile long before the Babylonians appear.

Our Western Danger

The above analysis is of course wrought with certain difficulties. Concerning Scripture it may court the danger of psychologizing. I have spoken of the persons of David and Solomon but I mean to refer to the cultural moods which these two persons seemed to have evoked and created, and which they certainly came to represent in the tradition. I happen to believe that the tradition is faithful in this reflection but that is not the point here. Concerning the value placed upon the two persons and regimes we have treated as models, this may sound like an attack on modern industrial life with Solomon used as a device for making a critique. But such is not intended. The alternative to the mercantilism of Solomon is not a nostalgic return to some romantic agrarianism, rather it is in David who participated fully in the urban world of his time but retained an awareness of the splendor of the life entrusted to him.

The models with which the tenth century provide us point to an important conclusion. David as presented in the tradition is a healthy model of the way a man can relate to "things" with the new freedom that technology has given us. On the one hand, he no longer grants things the power of magic and divinity which primitivism is inclined to do. In that sense he is emancipated. Thus David was free as Saul was not. But at the same time, he allows things to have a dignity, purpose, and place of their own which he is eager to respect and not destroy. This David did in contrast to Solomon who regarded neither persons nor things as having any meaning.

The process of secularization (which David embodies) must fight on both these fronts: freedom and respect. Two of the more important discussions of this subject have made a powerful case against the danger of treating things as divine.[3] But the danger of which they write is not particularly appropriate to American culture. As van Leeuwen has said, this is a struggle that is urgent for Eastern culture, which is hampered by a lack of creation-theology in the Eastern religions.

Our Western danger lies in the opposite direction, and of this neither Cox nor van Leeuwen have written with the same power.[4] Our danger is the danger of Solomon: we may become so impressed with our freedom and power and be so concerned to empty things of divinity that we shall empty them of meaning. Our problem is not that we tend to yield our sons to demonic gods as Saul almost did, nor that in our fear we conjure up the dead because we think we can't handle things. Just the opposite. We are so much the master, so much in charge that we cut babies in half to have "justice" as Solomon proposed. We sell people into slavery because of our program of expanding affluence. The result is the same as that of Solomon: we are bored; bored by things, by power, by our ability to control. Perhaps like

Solomon we shall find most of the kingdom taken from our hand because we have abandoned God (1 Kings 11:33).[5]

David in his freedom preserved what Solomon missed completely. David understood the preciousness of all life and so related to his fellows with an extraordinary awareness. Solomon regarded all of life as cheap and so saw his fellows at his disposal for his own arbitrary uses. David and his company understood the majesty of all of life and preserved an amazement about the world of things. Solomon understood only his own majesty and nothing of the majesty of life, so he was amazed at nothing in the world of things except as another commodity to be bought or sold. David understood the limits to his freedom. Even if he transgressed he understood the givenness of life, the mysterious dimension not subject to our management of manipulation. Solomon erroneously regarded his freedom as absolute, showed no respect for any givenness and was apparently insensitive to the dimension of mystery. Surely the story of the tower of pride (Gen. 11:1–9) is offered with an eye toward the lifestyle of Solomon.

Our danger in Western culture is not that we shall revert to the style of Saul and sell out our freedom to the gods. Perhaps that is the danger elsewhere, as van Leeuwen has seen. For us the temptation is Solomonic, adopting the new freedom and ingenuity of our fathers but forfeiting the sense of the holy which is discerned in the world of men and things—the sense which keeps us sane and lets life occasionally be a celebration.

As One Having Authority

The men around David discerned in him a new sense of authority and responsibility for his world such as Saul and his generation would never dare to grasp or claim. In David's own time this authority comes as "to till and to keep." In the later reflection it is "to have dominion." But it means the same in both the early and late traditions. In reflecting on the royal status of man as embodied in David it was seen as it had not been in Saul, that man is not subject to the whims of the gods, that he does not exist simply to appease and please them. Man has his own life to live, his own decisions to make, his own world for which he is responsible. David understood this clearly. He did not

cop out. He never asked the gods to make his decisions for him. He
was prepared to answer for the world entrusted to him.

In the midst of his being king and having the world for his own
use, David still knew himself to be a part of a fractured world, a world
in which death still came in unaccommodating moments (2 Sam.
12:15–23; 18:31—19:4). He still knew himself addressed by a prophetic word which he was prepared to hear (2 Sam. 12:1–14; 24:
10–14). He still knew that in his power he was a man sustained by his
fellows and needful of their support (2 Sam. 17:27–29; 1 Kings 2:7).
David had arrived at the delicate balance so that he did not abdicate
as Saul had done, nor did he "overreact" as Solomon was to do.

David and his contemporaries discerned that man did "have
dominion," but it was and is a curious kind of lordship with a relationship to "thous" and not to "its." It is mastery which places the master
in a caring relationship over his domain. It is also a sovereignty which
places the sovereign in some sense at the disposal of his subjects. It
is a theory of kingship which affirms that the king exists for the sake
of the kingdom. Of course, there is evidence that David was not
consistent with this understanding of himself, but it quite clearly is his
guiding principle.

Solomon could not understand the nuances of such a delicate
notion of power. He took "have dominion" as a one-dimensional
statement at face value. He exploited it so that everything became an
"it," even what should have been clearly "thou." He understood his
mastery as tyranny with no caring for his domain involved. He lived
his sovereignty in a despotism demanding that the kingdom exists for
the sake of the king.

Solomonic man urges us to live as David never was tempted to
do. Writing in a quite different context, Abraham Heschel says:

> Fellowship depends upon appreciation, while manipulation is the
> cause of alienation: objects and I apart, things stand dead, and I am
> alone . . . Reality is equated with availability; what I can manipulate
> is, what I cannot manipulate is not. A life of manipulation is the
> death of transcendence.
> . . . .
> Prior to the discovery of Nature's submissiveness to the power
> of man, man is clearly aware that nature does not belong to him.
> The awareness of nature's otherness precedes the awareness of

nature's availability. However, as a result of letting the drive for power dominate existence, man is bound to lose his sense for nature's otherness. Nature becomes a utensil, an object to be used. The world ceases to be that which is and becomes that which is available. It is a submissive world that modern man is in the habit of sensing, and he seems content with the riches of thinghood.[6]

That world is now a grave temptation to us in the West. It was a like temptation to David and to Solomon. David found resources to choose life amidst such options. Solomon abused Israel's moment of freedom and in an instant it had passed. No wonder he was left only to say, "Vanity of vanities, all is vanity" (Eccles. 1:2). Israel's moment of freedom was a brief one, between the fear of Saul and the tyranny of Solomon. It was David's moment when Israel discerned the meaning of faith, of freedom, and of the holy.

The Faith of a King

Each of these kings was a man of faith, and in each case his notion of faith and his theological perceptions corresponded to the way he related to his cultural context. In thinking through the theological stance of these kings and the world view each came to represent, I have found it useful to identify in symbolic terms their relation with Yahweh and therefore to suggest models under which their self-understanding can be presented. This self-understanding applies not primarily to the specific man but to the cultures over which he presided.

1. Saul is presented as the *obedient servant.* He is much concerned with the will of his God and seems preoccupied with honoring that will. The cultural situation to which this corresponds is one of legalism and superstition, a restrictive society of rules, obligations, and obedience. In Saul's time it is precisely expressed in the fear before his vow, in his fear before defeat, and perhaps also in the tragic depression that finally immobilized the king and destroyed his order. In our time that cultural mood is expressed in the mood of anger and fear which is variously termed "hard hat" or "silent majority" and which is concerned with "law and order." It is a cultural mood which is seriously religious, scrupulously moral, and passionately obedient, but settles for the role of servanthood, cut off from the joy and

freedom which it never risks attaining. In Saul's Israel and in our time, persons and social institutions struggle to be worthy servants and are also cut off from joy and freedom.

2. Solomon is presented as the *abandoned orphan.* He and his cultural mood have left home, abandoned all the old values, and so find themselves rootless and alone. They have gone partly in rebellious anger and partly in the celebration of newly found freedom and power. But either way they are now left alone with their ingenuity and shrewdness, their cynical capacity to control, and their great appetite for production and expansion. They are alone, without a place to rest, without a partner in dialogue, and as they deal only in commodities they become nameless commodities, orphans without a home, sons without a parent, men without a family.

3. David is presented as a *free, mature son.* He is not a slave living in fear or cowering obedience, nor is he an orphan who has left home to be free. He is a son who knows his father wills for him responsible freedom, trusting his world to him, holding him accountable, but finally letting him work it out. His is not a father who nags nor one who abandons, but one who stands by in confidence. The son is not one who must cower in adolescent obedience or rage in adolescent freedom, but who can instead grow to mature manhood because he knows his father calls him to it (cf. Eph. 4:11–16).[7]

Such a way of presenting these three historical persons and cultural contexts as theological models is of course problematic. I risk it because in large scope such models are faithful to the witness of the tradition. Saul's culture did destroy itself in fear. Solomon's culture was judged for its greedy autonomy (cf. Matt. 6:29). And Jesus emerged as the type of the new David, the one who took his manhood freely and seriously, faithful to his father.

In this connection, the story of the so-called prodigal son (Luke 15:11–32) is illuminating. The older son is the pure servant type, never experiencing sonship. The younger, when he returns, thinks he must be a servant but the pronouncements of the father are clear. He will not permit his son to settle for the easier, joyless role of servant: "This my son was dead, and is alive again; he was lost and is found" (vs. 24). The Solomon model is not represented in the story, because the Lukan tradition and Jesus' teaching generally was concerned with the other problem—dutiful, restrictive obedience, embodied in un-imaginative legalism. Indeed, the Solomon model corresponds pecul-iarly to a modern reality. If there had been a third son to represent the Solomonic model, I suggest he would still be in a far country, having forgotten the name of his father and the location of his home. Clearly, these models in Jesus' story and in Israel's history show that Yahweh's will for his man, his king, his people, is the embrace of mature manhood and mature sonship.

Wisdom theology is primarily concerned with our relationship to our environment. It encourages free and responsible use of it. David accepted that responsibility and the freedom of which the wisdom teachers spoke. Solomon also paraded his wisdom but it was wisdom gone flat and tyrannical, understanding freedom but not mystery, mastery but not responsibility. Wisdom warned against not asserting self, but it also warned against the arrogance embodied in Solomon. Perhaps it is that warning which is now most appropriate in the technological West.[8]

V.
The Meaning of Maturity for Current Theology

Our analysis of Israel's moment of maturity under David and her subsequent autonomy under Solomon has offered us models for understanding our own cultural context and our theological task. On the one hand it will not do in our time to aim at being *obedient servants* motivated by fear after the fashion of Saul, for such a stance is wholly out of touch with the demands and opportunities of our situation. It is equally clear that we cannot set the *abandoned orphan* as our model after the fashion of Solomon, for the abuse of power, knowledge, and technology for selfish ends—combined with abdication of responsibility—has already brought horrible troubles upon us.

The present time calls us to a remarkable maturity, free to celebrate, decide, and act, yet always free in the context of a father who trusts us and holds us responsible, who calls us by name and thus bestows on us the identity so essential to maturity. This Davidic model, reflected in a variety of ways in Israel's literature to which we have referred, is a viable and important one in our current theological work.

In theological discussion of the last decade we seem to have passed through a series of fads which have enjoyed remarkable and sudden popularity and disappeared with equal suddenness. However, the uneasiness and yearnings which led to these fads and the questions which they have raised continue to be urgent and nagging. The disappearance of the extreme popularity of a theological idea in no way disposes of the questions which it seeks to address. In one way or another, each of these enterprises (to which reference is made in what follows) is an attempt to respond to the call to maturity which our cultural situation presses upon us.

In what follows, I shall explore the thesis that *the major point of contact between each of these efforts and the Bible is to be found in the wisdom traditions.* I do not argue that other parts of Scripture are irrelevant to these issues, but only that the wisdom materials present the most ready point of contact which will let us understand the issues being raised. The mood and stance of the wisdom traditions is not unlike that of these discussions. By focusing on the wisdom traditions, a serious exchange between biblical faith and current theological efforts is possible in a more significant and serious way.

Theology of the Secular

Secularization is no recent phenomenon in Western culture even though it has become a popular and recognized notion only recently. Obviously the radical changes represented by it will not go away simply because the currency of the idea and the word has been somewhat dissipated. Rather, secularization points to a remarkable set of changes in social values and norms which have been a long time in coming and which surely will become more pronounced in the future.

The meaning of "secularization" is difficult to define, but one can at least characterize its major aspects. It was Harvey Cox who attracted most attention to it in theological discussions, and his characterization continues to be a useful one:

> We experience the universe as the city of man. It is a field of human exploration and endeavor from which the gods have fled. The world has become man's task and man's responsibility. Contemporary man has become the cosmopolitan. The world has become his city and his city has reached out to include the world.[1]

Central to Cox' statement is the stress upon the fact that the world is now man's task and responsibility (and elsewhere he adds, man's freedom). History has become man's enterprise and vocation.

The other, more popular presentation of the theological dimensions of contemporary social change has been that of Arend van Leeuwen. He has interpreted secularization in terms of technological power and freedom to analyze, plan, control, and organize.[2] This particular gift and capacity of the West he contrasts with the "ontocratic" East in which the world is understood in categories which exclude human freedom, power, or responsibility. Like Cox, van Leeuwen stresses the emergence of the human agent as the primary factor in secularization.

Behind Cox and van Leeuwen there is a long history of thought. Here we mention only two of the more formidable authors. In American thought, H. Richard Niebuhr has been a foremost theologian of the secular, though he does not particularly stress the word. In his *Radical Monotheism and Western Culture* he also observes that history and nature have been freed from all the little gods which have kept life "sacred" and keep man bound to special times and places:

> Radical monotheism organizes the sense of the holy in an another fashion. Its first effect is the consistent secularization of all those symbolic objects that polytheism and henotheism meet with sacred fear and joy . . . When the principle of being is God then he alone is holy and ultimate sacredness must be denied to any special being. No special places, times, persons, or communities are more representative of the One than any others are. No sacred groves or temples, no hallowed kings or priests, no festival days, no chosen communities are particularly representative of Him in whom all things live and move and have their being . . . The counterpart of this secularization, however, is the sanctification of all things. Now every day is the day that the Lord has made; every nation is a holy people called by him into existence in its place and time and to his glory; every person is sacred, made in his image and likeness; every living thing, on earth, in the heavens, and in the waters is his creation and points in its existence toward him.[3]

The secularization that Niebuhr writes of is perhaps not as extreme as Cox suggests, because Niebuhr never suggests the autonomy of man of which Cox hints. Rather, it is the end of the sacral as a possessive force which lets us experience the holiness which pervades all of life. It is the end of the boundary between sacred and profane which means not only the end of the tyranny of the sacred, but also the end of the void of the profane. Cox is now concerned with the latter in his more recent book *Feast of Fools*. Cox apparently concludes that in the technological West our crucial problem is not the sacral but the profane. Niebuhr had not stated the case for secularization as radically as Cox later did, and therefore has characteristically maintained a better balance. For Cox it has been necessary that *Feast of Fools* redress the onesidedness of *The Secular City*.

The other writer who has been extremely influential in this discussion, and to whom Cox acknowledges his indebtedness, is Friedrich Gogarten. Taking his clue from the slave/son images of Galatians 4:1–7, Gogarten has understood biblical faith in terms of the emergence of the mature son, responsible to God and responsible for the world, out of his servanthood which was devoid of responsibility.[4] It is clear that in much subsequent discussion the later motif of responsibility for the world has been stressed to the neglect of the former, responsibility to God, but the power of biblical faith as Gogarten understands it suggests that responsibility to God and for the world are held together in the exercise of mature sonship. It is this balance which Cox recovers by holding his two discussions together.

Each of these authors discovers in biblical faith a drive toward secularization, and especially Cox and van Leeuwen credit the biblical tradition with major influence upon that development in Western history. While that is in part true, it is important to recognize secularization as a sociological development related to the collapse of the dominant sacral symbols of another age. Secularization has had both positive and negative impact on biblical faith as it has been transmitted to us. On the one hand, the Reformation may be regarded as a crucial event toward secularization. It was a vigorous recovery of the biblical symbols which called into question the sacral-profane dualism of the earlier period. The connection of Reformation with secularization enables us to see the positive theological aspects of secularization. But on the other hand, it can also be argued that the very biblical symbols utilized in the Reformation held on to a social view of life which was judged a failure. Thus the Renaissance, the rise of scientism, and finally the Enlightenment may be viewed as a protest against such social symbols. Then secularization is viewed as a rejection of a theological world view and therefore as a negative event. From the perspective of biblical faith, secularization seems to have both positive and negative dimensions.

Both Cox and van Leeuwen find in the central biblical symbols of Torah, creation, exodus, and Sinai the handles by which we may understand secularization and which in part has been an impetus to it. But it is equally clear that these symbols (with that of creation excepted) really belong themselves to a sacral view of reality in which the *intrusion* and authority of the holy in the realm of human affairs causes the decisive turn. Moreover, these traditions are powerfully shaped by influences of myth rooted in a sacral world view (e.g., the exodus as the conquest of chaos, the theophany of Sinai as the cataclysmic coming of the holy). There is an element of truth in the assertions of Cox and van Leeuwen, but it should be recognized that these fundamental symbols and traditions are not as radically secular as has been suggested.

I believe it is much more plausible to suggest that in the wisdom traditions of Israel we have a visible expression of secularization as it has been characterized in the current discussions. Wisdom teaching is profoundly secular in that it presents life and history as a human enterprise. To the extent that wisdom was concerned with the preparation and education of the young in the court for positions of responsibility and power, such a stress is to be expected. Thus, wisdom is concerned with enabling potential leaders to *manage* responsibly, effectively, and successfully. It consistently places stress on human freedom, accountability, the importance of making decisions, and using power prudently and intelligently.

No potential king can be taught that he can trust his power to the gods, nor that the priests can make state decisions or shape public policy through ritual activity. It will not do for men of power to flee to the sacral. Though the office of king is hedged about by ritual and mythical claims, the day-to-day exercise of the office depends on his ability to cope, decide, and manage. He cannot abdicate these burdens and options by appealing to any sacral alternative. He has the power of his office and he alone is answerable for it. Clearly, wisdom in the court was hardheaded and uncompromising in maintaining such an approach.

For that reason, retribution teaching which looms so large in wisdom teaching is in fact an expression of this notion of secularization—that history is man's task and responsibility.[5] Retribution teaching is an expression of the conviction that man, especially the man of power, is accountable—that he must answer for and live with the consequences of his choices. The contrast between this approach and that of the more mythically-oriented historical traditions is clear. The latter, which express a more familar theology of grace, characteristically report the intrusion of God to the rescue, as in the exodus. By contrast, wisdom does not anticipate such an intrusion but holds man to the choices he makes. Such a firm conviction about retribution belongs with secularization as we have described it. Retribution theology as found in the wisdom teachings is a warning that one cannot flee to the sacral for escape from the results of foolish actions and choices. In this teaching, freedom and accountability belong together.

The emergence of wisdom in Israel is difficult to date, but there can now be no doubt that it came to vigorous expression in the midst of the David-Solomon period. Without being simplistic, I suggest an important parallel between the emergence of wisdom in post-Saul Israel and the emergence of secularization in the post-Christendom West. Wisdom was important in the former context of urban affluence precisely because the ancient symbols which were still adequate for Saul had collapsed. Appeal to the Torah of Sinai and the intruding God of the exodus were ineffective and disfunctional because they did not make contact with the new situation of power and freedom which called men to responsibility. In that situation, so parallel to our own, wisdom offered a way of faith which took the new situation seriously and recognized the human scope of the United Monarchy in ways that the old traditions did not and could not.

In commenting on Cox and van Leeuwen above, it was noted that of the traditions to which they appeal in relating biblical faith and secularization, creation is singularly different from the cluster of traditions which had serviced the Saul community. Creation faith as it is expressed for example in Genesis 2:4b–25 is a new affirmation in tenth-century Israel. While expressed in mythological form it is secular because it is concerned with the primacy and dominance of man over his world. Though this tradition is cast in the form of myth, its drive and intent are linked to wisdom: it is concerned with the freedom, power, and responsibility of man to manage his world.

The discussions of secularization mentioned above have not noted the distinctiveness of this tradition although it is quite different in terms of tradition history. Creation is not just another act of the saving God of the exodus. It is rather a very different way of perceiving man in the world because it affirms that man is responsible to God for the world. The uniqueness of the creation tradition relates to our theme of wisdom because it is closely linked to wisdom. It does not present man in needful helplessness, but in a powerful capacity to manage the world.

The current discussions have stressed that secularization is not profanation. It does not refer to the autonomy of man as though he were totally independent or totally abandoned. Rather, he is free in the context of God's trusting him. The wisdom traditions, often termed humanistic, pragmatic, and prudential, never questioned the notion that ultimate control of the world is not given into the hands of man, that he cannot finally know it all, that the inscrutable operation of life is not simply our ignorance to be dispelled by more study but it is mystery to be honored and celebrated.

Wisdom is powerful as an intellectual enterprise precisely because it holds together the freedom and responsibility of man with the real, though never intrusive, rule of Yahweh. If it is true that the profane and not the secular is our great threat in Western society, then it is this ability of wisdom to affirm the holy in the secular which can again be our teacher. Wisdom affirmed that "always man is totally in the world and always he has totally to do with Yahweh."[6]

Situation Ethics

A second current form of the theological discussion concerning our call to maturity is situation ethics. The most popular expression of that concern appears in two books by Joseph Fletcher,[7] the first of which caused the greater ripple, though the second was by far the more substantive. The particular form of the first book was unfortunate, because it seemed to some that the issue concerned primarily, or even exclusively, sexual freedom. Of course the reaction was predictable.

But the issue of situation ethics has continued after the popular stir over Fletcher's book disappeared. It continues in the more serious discussion among theologians who struggle with the question about the relation between principles and contextualism both in ethical theory and in practice. More importantly, it continues in the lives of persons and communities who daily experience new forms of freedom they don't understand and are ill-prepared to cope with. People feel a kind of nostalgic gratitude for the disappearance of old norms which they were possibly never convinced about in the first place. They look about for guides and probe boundaries which will not be simply a return to old patterns of restrictive obedience.

There are many reasons for the crises involving ethical guidelines, rules, and freedom. These include the new dimensions of technical knowledge which let us predict and therefore avoid the consequences of choices which in other times we did not understand so could not avoid. This applies to sexual mores as well as to other forms of social interaction. Our knowledge explosion has in some ways greatly simplified and yet greatly complicated our decision making. In any case, it has radically changed it. We now do not have to choose right or wrong ignorantly or blindly.

A far greater factor in the process of change has been the new understandings of human personality which stress actualization and self-realization. It is increasingly affirmed that full personhood is not achieved by obediently accepting norms, but by the cultivation and expression of the distinctive qualities of the person, even when the result is expression in radically new directions. This has been given a major impetus by so-called third force psychology, and comes to visible expression in such phenomena as the Human Potential Movement and the Women's Liberation Movement. In such contexts the old rules, principles, and patterns obviously are called into question, and what used to seem "right" now often seems to be simply restrictive and inhibiting.

The reasons for the change are sociological as well as psychological. We are, because of the malfunction of most of our major institutions, experiencing the questioning of almost every form of structural authority. Old authorities in home, school, government, military—in every area of public life—seem often not to understand new situations and certainly cannot cope with them. Thus their teaching authority is called into question and it is inevitably asked: if they are this ineffective, why accept their notions of right and wrong? Why should a dean be taken seriously if he has come to terms with the military establishment? Why should laws be obeyed when they are simply alibis for oppression and injustice? Why should parents be heard when their own lives express so much that is deceptive? The questions go on and on until those in authority earn the right to be heard.

Put in larger scope, the movement from a folk culture to an urban culture—from a stable, ordered community where yesterday's conclusions still make contact with today's circumstances, to a busy, crowded, mobile, fluid context where no patterns seem to endure—all this has set the old ethics in question. Such circumstances create questions about one's self, for the ways we had always thought to be "right" now seem only fatiguing, occasionally silly, and habit. There seems no good reason to keep at it in those ways. On every side there seems ample reason for no more business as usual.

When all is shifting and nothing seems certain it is not difficult to conclude that there is only me and my decisions, my fellows and their decisions, and our intention to treat each other in at least a decent way, if not a "human" way (whatever that means). In a context when all order seems to have failed, leaving us desperate or free or perhaps both, we may and must create an order for ourselves. We create it as we go, decision by decision.

Fletcher and those engaged with him have grasped the radically new situation in which we find ourselves filled with either despair or exhilaration. In that context Fletcher has proposed propositions which characterize a viable ethical stance:

> Only one thing is intrinsically good, namely love; nothing else.
> The ultimate norm of Christian decision is love; nothing else.
> Love and justice are the same thing, for justice is love distributed.
> Love wills the neighbor's good whether we like him or not.
> Only the end justifies the means; nothing else.
> Decisions ought to be made situationally, not prescriptively.

Fletcher's work (which perhaps needs to be toned down in the more sober context of Nixon's seventies, for it no doubt contains flamboyant elements) is an attempt to deal responsibly with a situation in which set norms seem either not valid or at least not compelling. His discussion could come only in a time when the traditional norms of a stable culture have lost their power.

There can be little doubt that wisdom also sought to deal with such a context when simple answers were inadequate. Currently it is held that wisdom had one of two social settings. Possibly it belonged to a large family grouping in which the older members responsible for the family, especially the father, instructed the young in the ways, actions, and choices which would create and sustain the well-being of the family. Alternatively, wisdom belonged to the court in which young men were educated to exercise the powers of the state. In either case (and the two are not mutually exclusive), such instruction was profoundly goal-oriented. In the family one teaches for the well-being of the family. In the court school one teaches for the life and prosperity of the realm.

Such teaching, because it is goal-oriented, is extremely pragmatic and contextual. One does not always do the same thing in the family, because the well-being of the family demands different actions and choices depending on circumstances. The same is true of the kingdom. (We have ample evidence of what happens when public policy clings to old ideological norms which no longer square with the realities, e.g., we are a long time getting free of the obsolete dogmas of the Cold War.)

Such instruction, in family or in school, was not committed simply to the communication of a set of propositions in catechetical fashion but in the setting of boundaries and guides within which actions could be made. The wisdom materials are remarkably free of dogmatic assertions which claim enduring validity. Rather, they are presented with a kind of tentativeness which claims only that for now is this the way it is, or seems to be.

The mood and method of the wisdom teacher was simply to make observations on the actions and choices which for that situation moved things toward "life." Such actions and choices might be generalized, for they surely also applied to other situations as well, but there is characteristically no insistence that they have enduring worth or ultimate authority. They claim our response only while they function to create "life."

Erhard Gerstenberger has argued with great persuasion that the commandment form, "thou shalt not," emerges from the older teaching to the younger, to protect and nurture the family.[8] Thus this most categoric and absolutist-sounding form is an instructional form designed for a specific ethical decision in a specific time. To be sure, over a period of time certain observations tested through many experiences came to be given special authority because they were shown to be correct in many cases. These turned out to be authentic boundaries to human freedom and action which could be honored in the interest of well-being. Those which proved such tests eventually were given sacral authority, as for example, in the Ten Commandments. But the sacral authority came later and is not really integral to the teaching.

It is sobering and important to remember that even the Ten Commandments (on such an understanding) emerged not from a mysterious finger on a holy mountain, but up out of a long experiential testing in the life of the community. Law in Israel seems characteristically to be derived from the situational practice of the wisdom teachers who shrewdly and patiently observed the actions which made for life.

When Fletcher's book first appeared, the author participated in a clergy symposium trying to understand it. After a heated, confusing discussion, one brother who did not understand but rejected it all concluded with the ultimate put-down. "I don't know about you, but I still believe the Ten Commandments." Little did he know that in that material, if Gerstenberger is correct, we have a classic example of situation ethics.

Out of the scholarship which is related to Gerstenberger's thesis several observations can be reported. First, every teaching expressing a simple imperative or prohibition, no matter how enshrined in authority, is rooted in and dependent on experience. We have found certain practices to be valid through experience and so we cling to them. Thus, situation ethics is a radically pragmatic approach to ethical norms. Second, the criterion for experience-tested norms is the goal—the creation of functioning community. Claims of validity are based not on the authority of God nor the sacral community, but on the well-being of the family, community, or realm. Third, only late and derivatively do the imperative and prohibitive forms claim any other authority of a structural kind. The functional authority of such ethical norms is that they produce desired results judged to be "good" in terms of our needs, wants, and objectives. They are never doctrinaire, insisting on a principle.

Such a way of determining right and wrong was particularly useful and appropriate in the heady context of power and freedom in the time of the United Monarchy. It was a time when the old authority probably was not functional, when it was risky business to suggest right and wrong to a king. (Although it did happen with Nathan [2 Sam. 12], I take that to be an exception.) For example, Proverbs contains observations about what will produce well-being in a realm (Prov. 14:28; 16:12; 20:28; 22:8; 25:5; 29:2, 4, 12, 14). Such teaching is no doubt contextual and is appropriate to the times and mood of the king.

Contextualism of course has its risks and is a one-sided view of the problem. In our time we have experienced the euphoric notion that the only moral values are those we choose and affirm. In the recent days of existentialism we have been tempted to think order was waiting to be created by us and that before us there were no givens. This is the extreme to which contextualism may be pushed, and when it is, its affinities with Israel's wisdom are ended.

As did Israel's kings, we are learning what the wise knew and continued to probe. There is something there before we decide it. There is an order to life. Boundaries exist which no amount of power, knowledge, or technological imagination can finally shift. Israel's kings had to learn repeatedly from the wise that oppression and injustice will destroy. This is not so because God revealed it or a prophet announced it or it stands in a holy book. It is just so because our experience has found it so (Prov. 29:4). In our time we are learning that sort of thing all over again.

> We are learning that one can utilize power to rape the earth so long, and then it is gone and there is only death.
>
> We are learning that after so much killing and plundering in the name of democracy something deathly happens not only to the bombed and killed people, but to the people who bomb and kill.
>
> We are learning that oppression of minorities finally catches up with us and we pay at least in fear if not in blood.
>
> We are learning, and here Fletcher directs most of his attention, that interpersonal relations geared to self-indulgence without any larger goals become empty, boring, and dehumanizing (cf. Prov. 25:16).

Wisdom is contextualism at its best, but it never falls into the trap of opposing contextualism to principles. It is contextual in that man is responsible and in each new situation he must make a fresh decision. It never suggests that all things are equally acceptable. It never believes for a moment that one can create his own world and pick and choose arbitrarily what we shall call "right" or "good." Our ethical freedom and our ethical responsibility take place in a world which is there before us. This world is the counterpole of our choices and actions. Wisdom dares to suggest that it is the greater partner in every ethical act, because finally this strange world which is different each day and defies our best reading, decides how it is with us.

The wisdom teacher confronted the king with this probably unwelcome reality: his ethical choices are not made in a vacuum nor in a world over which he presides. Rather, they are made in a world where all his power and all his knowledge changes things very little. This abiding givenness of the world which limits our options is seldom referred to by wisdom as the will of God. It is enough, given their empirical method and their non-authoritarian stance to say, "I have noticed that it is like that."

After a binge of existentialistic autonomy we are having to learn again the kind of situational ethics the wise understood, i.e., we are discovering the givens within which our freedom must operate. We may cite two examples. First, we are learning about the limits to freedom in relation to the abuse of our environment. Frederick Elder, in commenting on our active, aggressive abuse, proposes a new recognition of limits:

> In contrast to the status quo, and I would contend is a genuine alternative, is a position centering on restraint . . . there must be a deceleration in present trends. At heart is a position whose first question is not What shall be done? but rather What shall I not do? . . . If there is to be human survival, there must be a new era—one of restraint . . . Thus the new era will be a time of the "grand slowing down." . . . For though the fear of the Lord is the beginning of wisdom, it certainly is not the end of it. In the end, wisdom on the part of man in his relation to the rest of creation is made up of elements of harmony, symbiosis, respect for the integrity of nature apart from its utility for man, and within man himself, a humble, reverent, restrained spirit.[9]

This remarkable statement bears precisely on our theme. It holds for man being free to decide but it urges that man recognize the clear unalterable limits within which he must work and in which he must restrain himself. Finally, the perception of these limits is wisdom, which Elder describes as "man-nature wisdom."

In a second area, Norman Cousins writes of the propensity for commercial sexual exhibitionism:

> . . . an infallible formula has apparently been found for making sex boring. People who insist on seeing everything and doing anything run the risk of feeling nothing.

> It is a serious error to suppose that the depersonalization of sex is unrelated to other things that are happening to the society. The propensity for violence . . . the decline of respect for life . . . the casualness toward human hurt . . . the craving for heightened experience . . .—all these are symptomatic of desensitization. . . . What our society needs is a massive and pervasive experience in re-sensitization.[10]

Cousins, like Elder but in a quite different sphere, is attacking our seemingly unlimited freedom and urging a recognition of those limits beyond which we are choosing death. Both make their appeal without any claim of authority except the affirmation that life is like that, and all of our supposed freedom will not change reality.

In Israel's faith the creation traditions reflect on the moral context where man must live. He is given great freedom, but is hedged about by a tree he cannot approach, a tree of life around which he must move very delicately. As is well-known, the tree of life in the creation story is utilization of a wisdom motif (cf. Prov. 3:18; 11:30; 15:4). Thus Fletcher cannot be faulted for his stress on freedom and responsibility, but it is essential that this love or justice as a final norm is in a context of the ordering of creation which is not man-made and which man cannot void.

Such a stress cuts both ways. It reminds the rebellious with their adolescent style that the world didn't begin with their ethical freedom. It also reminds those who already have made up their minds and love the Commandments that the order is inscrutable, there is much we don't know and what we know is not at our disposal. In a recent discussion von Rad has shown that not only Job's friends who have answers, but Job himself is faithful to the wise tradition.[11] Wisdom is to know and to keep asking, to remember all our experiencing and to keep having new experiences. Situation ethics is a truly sapiential method, but the situation includes those remarkable boundaries which keep shifting and never yield to our pressure.

Theology of the Death of God

Again we consider a movement which at a popular level now claims little attention, but which raised persistent questions. The phrase "death of God" has of course been given a variety of meanings including the optimism of Hamilton, the philosophical, mystical turn of Altizer, and the torturous despair of Rubenstein.[12] To some extent these issues are dated, for in the seventies one is not likely to be as optimistic as was Hamilton in the Kennedy years. Nevertheless, they tell us something important has happened and is happening to our culture and to the ways we have of understanding ourselves.

Van Buren has surely provided a helpful beginning point in seeing the problem of "death of God" as a linguistic question related to a crisis in symbols. Again, it is the collapse of the medieval synthesis with its comprehensive symbol system which lies at the root of our problem. The notion of God in that circle of symbols had a positive content which gave moral and intellectual integrity to all of the experience of persons in Christendom—an integrity which was tied to the dramatic life of the church and its sacramental system. With the demise of that system as a meaningful dramatization of our experience and with the radically changing self-understandings that have arisen in the modern period, to speak about God is to utilize a symbol which has no correspondence to our experience. This radical change culminating in the secular experience of the Enlightenment placed man instead of God at the center of life, together with an appreciation of his enormous freedom and potential.

As van Buren and the others who expressed this concern recognized, we have arrived at a place where we must give up the use of that symbol, or we must recognize that we are using a symbol which appeals to a special sphere of life not having contact with our primary experiences. (Against this it can and has been urged that the symbol can conceivably have a more proper and primary role, but our purpose here is not to criticize the movement.) Given the irrelevant character of the symbol to those who wrote about it, two very different, indeed contradictory, moods appeared together.

On the one hand and more popularly, William Hamilton expressed profound optimism about an age of man in which the technological capacities of scientific man promised a world in which conventional appeals to God were impossible and unreasonable, as well as being unnecessary. To some extent, Altizer shared this view. The issue of God seemed to be set so that the freedom and greatness of man could be fully realized only through the death of God. Borrowing phrases from Bonhoeffer (apparently out of context) Hamilton expressed joy and celebration for the prospect of emancipated man.

At the other extreme and sharing very little with Hamilton except the formula, Richard Rubenstein has expressed a "death of God" theology with particular reference to the Jewish experience. As an epitome of his thinking he relates his experience in Berlin when a Christian leader took the position that Jews in Hitler's Germany suffered and died because they had sinned. By force of logic this must be so because the justice of God cannot be questioned or doubted. Rubenstein's reaction to this and to the entire effort to understand the Jewish holocaust in theistic terms is to conclude that it makes no sense to talk in terms of a God who in any way governs history, for what kind of God could be said to govern history and yet have this happen? Therefore, God is indeed dead. Man is alone and he must manage as best he can in a world which Rubenstein has described as a "jungle."

It is remarkable that such a movement under a single name can encompass both the euphoria of Hamilton and the despairing realism of Rubenstein. When we come to consider this movement with reference to our theme we must begin with the recognition that no piece of literature in Israel's wisdom corpus seriously entertains the notion of the death of God. At best we may seek points of contact and not more. But even if we seek only points of contact it is clear that we shall not find them in the salvation-history traditions. When one speaks out of these traditions one can only answer to the notion of "death of God," by saying, "he lives!" Such an affirmation may be true or meaningful, but it does not take seriously or understand the point of the assertion about the death of God.

Our point of contact must be elsewhere because the seeming dialogue with the salvation-history traditions is not a real one. It is to wisdom that we must look if the Bible is to seriously engage this attempt at understanding man's maturity in our current cultural context. It is precisely in the wisdom traditions that understandings of faith alternatives to the salvation-history traditions appear and boldly permit thoughts and words which are unwelcome in more official, orthodox circles. The literature of Job and Ecclesiastes represents the yearnings and weariness which could never receive a hearing in the primary traditions.

As points of contact and no more, I suggest these three moments in Israel's wisdom traditions:

1. The confidence in human freedom and choices characteristically found in Proverbs is not unlike the celebration of man expressed by William Hamilton. No specific text can be cited which puts the issue as Hamilton does, but Proverbs embodies the persistent conviction that man does have the capacity to choose wisely and to act toward life. This is fundamental to Proverbs, and without that assumption they make no sense.

It is no accident that von Rad persistently refers to this wisdom as set in a context of the "Enlightenment" of the United Monarchy, when the old symbols were not effective but when new human power and ingenuity were much in evidence. Hamilton's writings come from the Sputnik period of human confidence while the Enlightenment wisdom in Proverbs comes to Israel's awareness just at the time of Solomon's successes. Just as people are impressed with moon rocks in our time, they traveled some distance to marvel at this man come of age (cf. 1 Kings 10:1–10) who had successes comparable to our own space achievements. That also was a time of the king's freedom, power, and autonomy, when the whole world appeared to be under his control and subject to his will. It was also the time, as in our early 1960's, when man seemed able to do what he set his mind to.

While this version of "death of God" seemed to suggest that man's freedom and God's death belong together, wisdom in Israel seemed to affirm that even if talk about God is not terribly compelling, by whatever name it be called, man's freedom has its boundaries. There are limits that cannot be moved, barriers that may not be crossed without bringing death. Hamilton's death of God theology contained an important partial truth shared by Israel's wise, but they also affirmed what Hamilton did not: even in this radically human world maturity is not just our freedom to act. It also involves honoring the limits across which lies death.

Von Rad has shown that wisdom was able to celebrate the full coming of age of man, his emergence from minority, his new sense of responsibility, but wisdom also affirmed without apology faith in the rule of God.[13] It is that balance which characterizes the achievement of the wise which is lacking both in the older historical traditions and in recent death of God theology.

2. The death of God theology received a much more serious and compelling statement from Rubenstein, and although he found no joy in his conclusion he was forced to it by the logic of events. In Israel's wisdom traditions the dominant spirit of Proverbs belongs to the success and well-being of the tenth century, the beginning of the monarchy, while the poem of Job belongs probably to the sixth century—the end of the monarchy when all the grandeur and glory has vanished and Israel is left with only her troubles and her bitter memories.

The period of the exile and just before it was a time of radical disillusionment, perhaps symbolized by the unexpected and seemingly unwarranted death of Josiah in 609 B.C. From this period comes the bitter protests over the situation in Jerusalem when God seems to have forgotten it (Ps. 74, 79) and the weary despair of those in exile who had trusted and now seemed abandoned (Ps. 137). Most vividly in the Lamentations comes the desperation of the lost:

> She weeps bitterly in the night,
>   tears on her cheeks;
> among all her lovers
>   she *has none to comfort her.*
> She dwells now among the nations,
>   but finds *no resting place.*
> . . . her fall is terrible,
>   she has *no comforter.*
> Hear how I groan;
>   there is *none to comfort me.* (Lam. 1:2, 3, 9, 21)

In her laments Israel characteristically appealed either to her innocence or to Yahweh's faithfulness in spite of Israel's guilt. But now nothing matters. There is none to comfort!

Into this context comes the poem of Job, claiming his innocence, protesting his suffering and receiving no answer. The friends of Job, pure examples of orthodoxy, take the same role as Dean Gruber, the Berlin churchman, took toward Rubenstein in affirming the justice of God even at the expense of human need and hurt. The poem of Job presents the disillusioned sufferer waiting for help and the voice of orthodoxy giving bookish, irrelevant, proper answers.

The connections between Job and the work of Rubenstein are of course tenuous. Rubenstein has rejected such a connection claiming that the Jewish experience of recent time is much more radical and that it requires a total rejection of this universe of discourse which the poem of Job is still able to employ.[14] But Job never approaches any hint of the death of God. At the most, his God is absent or silent, but nothing more.

Nevertheless, both that ancient poem and this modern agony portray the experience of the collapse of an entire system of morality. The exile of Israel is indeed the end of that system of right and wrong upon which the prophets had based their message. And Rubenstein is speaking about the collapse of the moral system upon which western civilization has been premised. The endings are perhaps different. It is not clear where Judaism of Rubenstein's kind will end. Even the poem of Job ends in a perplexing way. But this much at least is clear: the move from Hamilton's optimism to Rubenstein's despair is not unlike Israel's movement from the celebration of the tenth century to the alienation of the sixth, from the buoyancy of Proverbs in its formative parts to the agony of the poem of Job. Whereas Israel's more orthodox traditions scarcely noticed either the buoyancy or the agony, wisdom responded to and struggled with these remarkable experiences which are not unlike our own contemporary extremities.

3. The resignation of Ecclesiastes corresponds to a growing mood in our time. So far as I know, no recognized theological writer has related the death of God idea to a response of futile indifference. Even if it has not received such professional, formal treatment, there is no doubt that the mood is among us, perhaps especially among caring believers who are weary.

It is expressed in the fatigue of liberals who have watched as the problems get bigger and bigger in spite of our best efforts. It is felt by caring churchmen who reluctantly conclude that nothing really is going to change. It is experienced by youth who must make decisions about their futures while wars and rumors of wars, and expensive, irrelevant education goes unchecked. It is the feeling of desperation that comes when in spite of best efforts nothing in public life is altered in any significant way.

No one has called such a widespread mood "death of God," but that is what it is. It is the feeling of hopelessness, the willingness to drop out, the absence of any viable symbol of hope around which to rally. The old symbols are powerless and inspire no courage. There is no expectation that anything is going to happen, that any intrusion will come to make things better. It is death of God in low profile, without an attempt to articulate it.

The mood corresponds to Ecclesiastes: ruminations of one resigned to a domesticated future. The piece is set in the Hellenistic period when all the power of the old Israelite tradition has disappeared. Now there is resignation, not terribly bitter, but knowing all the time that Godot will never come. It is a mood that had been expressed earlier:

> . . . those who say in their hearts,
> the LORD will not do good,
>   nor will he do ill. (Zeph. 1:12)

Only now it has become a way of life. This piece is relevant because it catches the mood of so many in our culture, too disillusioned to celebrate and too weary to protest. It is enough to survive.

These three great wisdom pieces in the Old Testament (Proverbs, Job, Ecclesiastes) are attuned to human experiences in the extremities as the salvation traditions are not. These pieces have no position to defend, no creed to protect. They know that what people experience is how it is with them even when it is not according to our wish for them. In our time, our formal, official religion has not caught up with the experience of our time. Perhaps it never can, but the wisdom traditions know some things the "official" traditions seldom learn. Among the most important of these is the admission that life as we must live it is often more lonely, sometimes more bitter, and occasionally more buoyant than our theology lets us affirm.

On Black and White Theology

In no area of theological discussion is the call to maturity more urgent than in the emergence of a Black theology which will be authentically Black and not simply an imitation of White theology. Martin Luther King, because of his personal power and because of the timing of his emergence in the Black movement, was able to make his theological appeal largely in terms of conventional theology without any radical break. He appealed to the symbols of the salvation history which have also fostered White theology.[15] One cannot of course know how King's theology would have developed had he lived, but it seems clear that any viable Black theology for the immediate future must be more radical than that which King formulated. It must very likely articulate a radical discontinuity with the ruling patterns if it is to break out of a theological Uncle Tomism.

It is not possible for a White author to contribute much to the task of reconstruction in Black theology. But with reference to Black theology the White community has a considerable amount of homework to do to discover how White our theology has been, and to discover ways in which we might get freed of some of the more offensive and crippling aspects of our White theology.

I understand "White theology" to be in a plantation context, i.e., designed to encourage obedience to and confidence in those who run the plantation.[16] I suggest it has functioned in at least three ways in our common life:

1. Most obviously it has been used by Whites to keep Blacks and other minority groups in subservience. Best known of course are the arrangements by which Negro slaves were promised heaven in the future for unquestioning obedience on earth.

2. The same style of religion has been used by the White establishment to keep all the brothers in line, White as well as Black. This has been possible because of the insidious alliances which are characteristically formed between the church and all other forms of power, so that it becomes a religious virtue to obey the government even if that government is corrupt and oppressive. It becomes a virtue to obey school authorities even if the whole operation is unfair and irrelevant. Eventually this alliance makes unthinking obedience the most prized of all virtues, and the promise of goodies in this world and/or the next is tied to that kind of obedience. Theology serves such an arrangement by making obedience the identifying mark of our humanness.

3. Finally, and most subtly, we have played the plantation game so long that we have done ourselves in by it theologically. The God with whom we think we have to do is imaged as "massah." In turn, our self-image is necessarily mean and low. Thus humility, meekness, and obedience are much sought after and prized. The self-giving nun is a pure product of that thinking. One can see the depth to which we

prize that symbol and some of the reasons why there is, for example, savage hostility when post-Vatican II nuns become involved in the issues of the day.

This plantation complex besets both Black theology with its Tom-obsession and White theology with its master-obsession, so that in Western culture we are all likely to be trapped in it, occasionally on both sides of the question. Among clergy and in other groups as well, the pattern of "passive-aggressive" behavior is frequent because we are boxed in by virtues of humility and meekness which correspond neither to our real selves nor to our professional responsibilities.

Moreover, it seems likely that biblical theology rooted in the salvation and the mighty deeds of God traditions is now deeply linked to a plantation theology in which we are in "Egypt" waiting for someone to help us, or we are at "Sinai" learning how to obey. Such attitudes are perhaps not the only ones that can be derived from these traditions, but for now these are the most likely options.

Here I suggest simply that the wisdom theology we have previously considered may provide a way free from such a plantation theology. We need not only changed institutions and changed social circumstances, but equally important, a changed self-image. We need no longer the model or self-image of the obedient slave, and we are in danger of rebounding to that of the autonomous orphan. The wisdom traditions offer another option: the model of the mature son living in a caring relationship with his brothers. These various models function whether we speak of Black theology or White theology, whether we incline to domination of or subservience to others. It is clear that in terms of self-understanding, Blacks and Whites who are trapped in a plantation mentality can only be freed from it together.

I have suggested some of the basic convictions of wisdom theology, and here explore their usefulness for a fresh approach to Black and White theology.[17]

Against wisdom theology's affirmation of the abundant life here and now, Blacks and Whites caught in plantation theology have engaged in living for deferred goals. The essence of conventional Black theology has been to sit still and wait and it will come later. The essence of conventional White theology is to focus on "spiritual matters," on questions of morality and obedience which amount to a baptism of the status quo. In effect, this has served to bracket out all the real social and material questions so essential for the abundant life.

The convenient upshot of this has been to support the White community in its unequal share of life's goodies. The comfortable split between a very spiritual religion and a very comfortable living circumstance serves to keep any important question from being raised. The White community has thus been freed from asking ultimate questions about the goodies, and the Black community was thereby encouraged to accept inequalities as a necessary prerequisite to something else which would hopefully be better. I know of no more vivid expression of that theology than the first question and answer in the old *Evangelical Catechism:*

> What should be the chief concern of man?
> Man's chief concern should be the eternal salvation of his soul.

Only a little better was the answer of the *Westminster Catechism:*

> Man's chief concern is to glorify God and to enjoy him forever.

Such a sequence brackets out all important questions for both Blacks and Whites and supports the White system by focusing on something remote from all our vested interests.

Obviously, the entire Bible protests against such a notion, but most clearly wisdom theology is less interested in eternal salvation of souls and more concerned about abundant life here and now. Wisdom theology can expose our special pleading in ways that can free us.

White theology has been committed to a strong, clear system of authority in which master commands and slave obeys. It happens in subtle ways and permeates all of our life:

> Don't run in church.
> Don't spit on the flag.
> Don't write in the Bible.
> Don't abuse property.
> Don't ask such questions.

Some such prohibitions may be of social value, but the result of structuring life this way is to create a stable, unchanging social context in which the present arrangement in all of its curious details takes on eternal value. In these prohibitions, the "flag" has little to do with patriotism and more to do with our present social system which sanctions certain inequalities. "Bible" here refers to no "live word" but to conventional morality given sacral authority to keep the kids off the street.

Such a value system in every area of social interaction attributes vast authority and control to people who keep our White world the way we like it. The way to survive in that world, or alternatively, the way to get to heaven, is to obey, to please, to appease, to be an Uncle Tom. Perhaps "Massah loves his colored," but in any case it's best to stay in your place.

Wisdom theology grants nobody that kind of authority. Kings rule not because they are kings, but because of wisdom (Prov. 8: 15–17). They must earn the right to authority. All authority is regarded functionally and never is it vested. The changed self-image derived from such a shift is that we become free to decide about authority. No one is due more authority than he merits by the way he functions. Such a notion is frightening to those of us in authority, but it is at least as liberating as it is frightening. The pressure toward Black Power and the right to self-determination, the right to have a say in one's own destiny, is fully consistent with such a functional view of authority.

White theology has always taught that "Massah knows best," whether it is we over slaves or God over us. Many writers have recently said we need a theology of change, or more radically, a theology of revolution. White theology is the pure type of antichange and antirevolutionary theology because it is a theology of irresponsibility. It has imaged a world which is eternally ordered, which God has called into being and rules, and into which it is our business to fit. If change must come, it is God's business and not ours.

Such a theology is big on relieving anxiety. It has told us not to worry, which inevitably comes to mean not to care. Every theology and every ministry which serves primarily to relieve anxiety invites people to accept things as they are. The end result is that we preclude questioning, protest, self-assertion, and civil disobedience. All of which is very nice if one happens to be White.

Against that, wisdom teaches consistently that our choices matter, that we must choose and decide, that we are called to shape our society, manage our world, and choose our destiny. Against all abdication, wisdom calls for caring action which of course comes to mean in this context Black Power. It is intended that every man be a man of power, free to assert himself and have a share in the future. Black Power, where it is in the interest of responsible community, is a faithful embodiment of wisdom theology. Such Black Power affirms that we are not passive recipients of our future but responsible for it. Such a theology is a judgment on every social structure and institution which nurtures men to abdicate as plantation theology always does. So often church, school, and government engage in such nurture.

White theology has by practice and perhaps by design given men low self-esteem. It has kept folks humble and obedient—not feeling too good about themselves—for such a self-image reduces self-assertion. White theology has produced persons who feel most comfortably abdicating: "After all, I'm only human." In every phase of life, with people of every color, this theology reduces persons to "boy" or "nigger."

Wisdom theology of course will have none of that. It treats man like a king: valued, powerful, and free if he is to accept the responsibility wisdom places upon him to choose life for himself and his fellows. Translated in terms of Black theology, it means: "Black is beautiful," or in any theology, "I am beautiful." Wisdom theology makes sense only with people who love self enough to care and to celebrate. Then perhaps even frightened plantation owners can come to say, "White is beautiful, so beautiful we do not need a nigger to tell us what we cannot believe." Too much our theology is grounded in self-hate. Wisdom is a call to self-love and thence to brother-love. That's how it is with mature sons, but cannot be with obedient yet fearful servants.

Wisdom theology, I submit, can be an important source for Black theology by articulating a way for persons of maturity. But it is equally important for white persons who are also boxed in by a plantation mentality. Both the owners and the niggers are boxed in, in the same box, and only together will they get free enough to own their sonship.

A variety of pressures have called these discussions to expression. But in one way or another, each of them is struggling with the vocation of maturity which is in part required by our cultural situation, in part urged by our faith:

> Secularization asks us to embrace the world as a human world.
>
> Situation ethics asks us to be reasonable in decision making when our freedom runs beyond our guidelines.
>
> Death of God theology asks us to live with our freedom and agony when conventional ways of referring to God seem doubtful.
>
> Black and White theology urges us to abandon our plantation mentality.

Our cultural situation and our faith will keep on making these demands.

Up to this point the Bible has played a minimal role in these discussions. But when the call to maturity is seen as the focal point of these efforts and when the wisdom traditions are considered as a point of contact, these theological explorations—even if they seem outside the scope of conventional theology—are not discontinuous with biblical faith. They can utilize biblical materials in a variety of ways to come to terms with the call of the biblical God that we be neither servants nor orphans, but grateful sons and daughters. It is a call that is always frightening and glorious. It is demanding and surprising. We don't know what to make of it, because our history has for so long given us other models for faith and for life.

VI.
The Wise Man as a Model for Ministry

This call to maturity, experienced in ancient Israel in her time of Enlightenment and reflected in much current theological activity, poses important questions for the ministry. How does our ministry reflect this call to maturity? How does the ministry of the church relate to persons and institutions who are struggling with the call to maturity. How does the ministry itself get shaped in mature ways?

The recovery of these neglected parts of Scripture and the emphases in current theological discussion noted above are a part of the crisis of ministry now widely felt. That crisis of course relates to the function and task of the whole ministry of the church. What does mission mean when the old paternalistic habits of foreign missions are unwelcome and increasingly ineffective? Or when the institution fails to claim any central position in social organization as it has in the past?

The confusion and crisis is even more urgent and acute for the professional practice of ministry. What does it mean to those who propose to engage in ministry in a professional way? This confusion about function and the failure of our usual understandings are reflected in the widely publicized dropouts among Roman Catholic priests and the unrest related to the rule of celibacy, as well as the increasing drop-out rate among Protestants.[1]

This confusion about our perceptions of professional ministry is not news, and clearly appeals to the conventional biblical models of minister as prophet and priest but do not greatly change our understanding. If anything, it only adds to our frustration and confusion.

One recent and helpful attempt to deal with this crisis is the intensive Danforth study of ministry in the context of the university.[2] Following normal theological patterns, even the conventional pattern of our understanding of the work of Christ, Underwood has settled on the models of prophet, priest, and king, as he explores the meaning of ministry. From these three models he posits four modes or functions of ministry, two being derived from the task of priesthood:

Priest:	1) ministry of counseling
Priest:	2) ministry of worship and proclamation
Prophet:	3) ministry of prophetic inquiry
King:	4) ministry of governance

The three classical scriptural models of ministry under which the work of Christ and the church have been understood, and to which Underwood appeals, have responded to *clearly articulated and expressly felt needs* in the community of faith.

1. The *priestly* ministry in Israel, concerned with sacrifice and intercession, dealt with the problem of sin and guilt and the felt need for *forgiveness and reconciliation.* This ministry has great power and significance where a proper relationship with God is valued. Moses as priestly model has great power and significance where a proper relationship with God is valued. Moses is valued in ancient Israel as an intercessor (Exod. 32:30–35) as he offers the appropriate sacrifices to make covenant possible (Exod. 24:1–9). So also Samuel (1 Sam. 12:19).

The priestly model has been primary throughout the history of the church's ministry. Much of the power of the Roman Catholic Church is grounded in the conviction that its priestly system deals effectively with the problem of sin and the reality of forgiveness. In contemporary Protestantism this same function is clearly a ministry in which many clergymen feel most comfortable. Current stress on counseling programs is a spin-off from the same concern.

2. The *prophetic* ministry was valued in Israel in relation to a felt need for *transcendent assurance and guidance.* The extended episode of 1 Kings 22 assumes that such guidance and assurance makes a difference to the king, though he has no direct access to them. A more pathetic example is the desperation of Zedekiah in relation to Jeremiah (Jer. 37:17; cf. also Ezek. 20:1–4). The reaction of Zedekiah and the drama of Jehoiachim (Jer. 36:23–25) suggest the enduring tension between the felt need and the inclination to resist the prophetic word —a tension rarely resolved. In such a culture, this function is taken as important for perceiving situations and making appropriate decisions.

3. The third model, the *royal,* meets the felt need for *order.* Israel's monarchy was designed to create order in the midst of the

persistent threat of chaos and disorder, both cosmic and political. Thus in the royal Psalms (e.g., 72) the king is the source of prosperity, fertility, justice, and well-being. Without him, the forces of death reappear. This is true even with King Jesus: in his death and absence chaos reappears (Mark 15:3, 38), but in his presence, chaos is controlled (Mark 4:35–41).

Each of these three models makes a *claim to authority and efficacy*. Each claims for itself the capacity to involve the holy in historical situations. They claim to speak and act for God, and the community for which they function affirms their efficacy and credits their authority.

The *priestly* office operates through sacrifice and intercession, sometimes in a simple and sometimes in an elaborate apparatus. The narratives about the various priestly orders in Israel concerning Aaron (Lev. 1:5, 8, 11), and the Levites (Deut. 33:10; cf. Exod. 4:10–17; 32:25–29; 1 Chron. 29:22) credit them with authority because of purity, knowledge, obedience, or ancestry. In any case, they make the system work and they are granted authority appropriate to their function.

The *prophet* is attributed remarkable authority in Israel. That authority, expressed in the messenger formula "Thus saith the Lord," affirms that he speaks not his own word but that of another who sent him. While some questioned and some resisted and some sought to analyze that authority (cf. Deut. 13:1–5; 18:15–22), it was generally accepted as a presence to be taken seriously.

The office of *king* of course claims a parallel kind of authority. The monarchy is not a historical accident nor a political necessity, but claims for itself sacral roots. It is the way in which life and well-being are guaranteed and the holy is visible in the community. Thus the king is the "lamp of Israel" (2 Sam. 21:17) or "the breath of our nostrils" (Lam. 4:20). The community in those traditions is deeply dependent upon the office and responds in loyalty and obedience.

In each case, the community gave *symbolic and dramatic sanction* to the claim and work of the office. Though the evidence is unclear, very likely some form of *ordination* was practiced as the community gave recognition to the authorization claimed from God. The priest of course had such credentials (Exod. 28:41; 32:29; Lev.

8:33; Judg. 17:5–12; 1 Kings 13:33), and in at least one case the priest is said to be "annointed" (1 Chron. 29:22). Such formal, dramatic acts reinforced the authoritative character of the office.

The case of the prophet is not as clear. Older scholarship spoke of "call narratives" (Amos 3:3–8; Isa. 6:1–8; 40:1–11; Jer. 1:4–10; Ezek. 1), which were literary efforts to establish authority. Recently H. G. Reventlow has suggested that because of their characteristic form and structure these narratives are literary deposits from formal public acts of ordination, thus stressing the symbolic sanction of the community.[3] Reventlow's hypothesis is a problematic one, but it suggests a possibility for understanding the community's acceptance of the office. Of course, in the great festivals of coronation and inauguration the king had a similar drama of public sanction, evidenced for example in the claim of Psalm 2:7 that the king is "God's son."

Thus the three offices, in terms of which ministry has been most often understood, include these elements:

> ability to deal with a felt need:
> > *Priest:* forgiveness and reconciliation
> > *Prophet:* transcendent guidance and assurance
> > *King:* order

> claim of authority and efficacy:
> > *Priest:* sacrifice and intercession
> > *Prophet:* "Thus saith the Lord"
> > > (to stand in the divine council)
> > *King:* sacral claim as source of life

> symbolic and dramatic sanction from the community:
> > *Priest:* ordination or annointing
> > *Prophet:* call or ordination:
> > > "The Word of the Lord came"
> > *King:* enthronement:
> > > "This is my son"

There are large and important areas of our cultural life where these models are adequate and effective, but there are increasing areas where these models are without any force, having become disfunctional and meaningless. While it may be argued that the failure of the models is related to the failure of biblical authority, it can be argued that Scripture, which offers another model, continues to have some impact where the models have failed. This is found in forms of counterculture such as the Black Power movement, the Berrigan protests, and some expressions of the Jesus people. Even if the use of Scripture is sometimes perverted it can provide powerful symbols.

For many people in situations of ministry these felt needs no longer give a basis for a life of faith or the practice of ministry. In a neat and well-known phrase Horst Symanowski has observed that forgiveness from God is not a high priority item for many people: the real question is not "Where do I find a gracious God?" but "Where do I find a gracious neighbor?"[4] Thus the priestly function is not taken very seriously.

Similarly, with our amazing technological competence the need for transcendent guidance and assurance is no longer very important or much felt. It is affirmed that we have the resources and capacity to manage very well, and in any case, a prophetic figure can't really speak relevantly to the complex technological questions all confused with moral issues. Gustafson has made clear the need for technical competence if one hopes to address the important issues seriously.[5] Clearly the need for technical competence is more valued and effective than a general religious concern or an intense moral passion. Our conventional models for ministry naturally and inevitably stress our religious concern and moral passion. That is what those models intend to embody. But they provide no intergral way to value technical competence in relation to ministry, indeed, by definition such models preclude it as a mark of ministry.

Surely the felt need for order which is related to the ministry of kingship is relevant only when the world feels chaotic in its deepest roots. To many affluent and successful people the world does not feel that chaotic, and even if it does, human energy and knowledge seem the best ways of coping with the problem. For many reasons, the felt needs around which conventional models for ministry have been constructed seem not very urgent.

In a similar fashion, old claims to authority are curiously unconvincing. The capacity of a priest to "make it right" hardly is persuasive even if perchance there is a concern to make it right with God.

Much restlessness among younger clergy and the collapse of authentic piety suggests that many clergy do not regard such authority or responsibility very seriously. When one no longer believes in the "power to forgive," the rationale for the traditional priestly office is gone.

The prophetic claim to speak God's word on any important question is at best problematic because the major issues are exceedingly ambiguous, and because when such attempts are made they are often rejected by the community of faith. Clearly, such words carry no authority beyond the personality of the speaker which confirms the loss of structural authority. Correspondingly, the role of kingship has lost all claim to authority. Whether one speaks of presidents, bishops, or teachers, structural authority has no clout and its claim to either the competence or responsibility for ordering the life of the community is generally questioned or doubted.

We need only add a note about the emptiness of dramatic and symbolic sanction from the community. Though the rites are practised, neither participants nor the witnessing community is much impressed—indeed, they cannot be. When the felt need is gone, when serious claim to authority and efficacy is no longer affirmed, then the formal sanction of the community is an empty charade and corresponds to no reality. Traditional models of ministry are beside the mark in such situations. Those who try to survive on conventional models in such situations are forced to scramble for power and authority inappropriate to their models. While the *functions* Underwood stresses continue to be important, the traditional *models* to which he appeals will not provide a starting place for understanding the functions.

Our concern is to explore an alternative model for ministry where conventional felt needs, conventional authority claims, and conventional symbolic sanctions have failed or collapsed. I suggest that ministry in such situations may appeal to the biblical model of the wise man, the confidant, and consultant to the man of power (the king) who could make few claims for himself but stood in a strategic position to put the right question or make the right observation to affect policy in significant ways.

It is extraordinary that in the history of Christian ministry this model has not been exploited, because in Israel it is the wise man, not the king, who represents the third structure of ministry along with the prophet and priest (Jer. 18:18). At this point I believe Underwood's study wrongly appeals to the king as model, for ministry normally is not by the one in power, but stands alongside the king. In our society for example, a corporation executive stands at the center of corporate power, knowledge, and influence. Indeed, he is involved in the kind of structural authority which has social force in our culture. If he is related to the church his professional minister relates to him in many functions. But realistically, it is the executive, not the minister, who exercises royal functions. The minister at best is alongside in what I suggest is the role of the wise man.

The model of wise man is appropriate in a cultural situation where the normally felt needs are not felt: a situation of relative *health* (in which forgiveness by God and reconciliation to God seem unimportant); a situation of *confidence* (in which transcendant guidance and assurance seem irrelevant); a situation of *power* (in which the king is able to cope, and chaos seems no pressing threat).

The "king" (the manager of great economic and political influence) as a man of continuous action has needs related not only to his person but also to the exercise of his office. Ministry is not simply to the *person* of the king, but to his *public* responsibilities. Men of power (and that means increasing numbers of middle-class Americans) need "question-putters" who can probe larger visions so that power does not become an endless cycle of having and getting more power. One continually engaged in coping responsibly with crises (and that includes increasing numbers of middle-Americans as they become more affluent) needs a reflective presence to discern hidden issues, to ask about obscure opportunities, to think through options and resources, and to ask about the relation between private and communal good. The person of power who lives beset each day with massive and dangerous issues has no time for the luxury of the question of meaning, but the question is no less important for that reason. Ministry has the opportunity to be at the right place at the right time with the compelling vision and the appropriate question or reflection.

This ministry will surely become more important. The awareness of what technology is doing to us, the difficulty power people have in understanding and communicating with the restless ones, the new sensitivity to the rape of consumerism, all suggest a climate in which larger issues and more far-reaching visions have a chance of being taken seriously. The wise man is the one with the finesse and shrewdness to put the question of meaning in ways that do not irritate the king. He is equipped to make observations out of experience so that the king must share the insight as his own. The wise man serves to help persons of power probe the options and explore the limits beyond which our power brings death rather than life. He responds to the *felt need for perspective.*

In suggesting this model I mean to suggest not only a way of ministry but a context of ministry. The wise man has his reason for ministry *vis-à-vis* the king; only in this is wisdom important or meaningful. In Israel, wise men functioned persistently and precariously in the king's presence. This ministry is appropriate precisely in the places where decisions are made which mobilize great power in far-reaching ways.

In that context the question of authority and efficacy takes a different shape. Because it is a ministry of insight which emerges from below rather than from above it makes *no claim to transcendent authority.* It has no commission, speaks for no other, has at its disposal no special power to achieve anything. What it has going for it comes from below, not from above. It relies only on the power to penetrate, the capacity to discern, the shrewdness to see clearly and deeply when others do not. Thus it has no authority other than a functional one; no appeal beyond the authenticity of its insight.

It follows that there also is no *symbolic sanction* to which the wise man can point. Because his claim is functional and his authority pragmatic he has nothing to which to appeal as sanction other than his effectiveness in seeing clearly and reflecting honestly. It is a ministry which is content to have the symbolic power rest always in the king, content with an apparently modest but most crucial role: enlarging the vision out of which the king makes his choices, thus opting for the life or death of the whole society.

Continuing the components we outlined earlier:

ability to deal with a felt need:
> *Wise man:* reflective presence to probe larger issues and discern boundaries

claim of authority and efficacy:
> *Wise man:* ability to discern truly

symbolic and dramatic sanction from the community:
> *Wise man:* the pleasure of the king

This analysis does not propose the wise man as the most effective or most desirable model for ministry, but simply describes what is likely to be possible in a situation where the other models no longer make effective contact. At best it is a study in feasibility.

The ministry of the wise man is indeed "ministry at the margin" of the faith community.[6] He is at the margin of sacral leverage, formal sanction, and authority. This ministry at the margin requires a different style and self-understanding.

The wise man is part of a team of which he is not the leader, nor is the life of the team conducted on his terms. His is a situation of pluralism in which questions of value and reality are wide open and unsettled. Such a placement of ministry calls for abandonment of all self-image and self-presentation of the minister. The focus of action is not upon him or his judgment or action but upon the issue at hand and the decision to be made. He must relate to that issue as best he can.

Similarly, "ministry at the margin" means that the characteristic concerns of the church also do not figure prominently (though a minimum of maintenance concern is inevitable). The conventional activities of the church will be at the fringe of the concern of this model because the real issues of power, justice, security, and order are not resolved in the church, but in the secular world where the wise man makes entry and gets heard because he talks sense.

The wise man in Israel has suffered from a caricature of calculating pragmatism. To be sure, the wise man is calculating and pragmatic, for only a fool does not calculate the consequences of his actions (cf. Luke 14:28–32), but it does not follow that the wise man in Israel is unprincipled and is guided by sheer relativism. It is abundantly clear that wisdom is an attempt to discern the character of the world as God has created it (cf. Prov. 16:2, 9; 19:21; 20:24; 21:2, 30). Wisdom speaks about the "givens" within which life must be lived.

The wise man knows that the world has a coherence which provides the context in which our decisions must be tested; that there are clear limits and boundaries which must be honored; that there are responsibilities which must be shouldered; that risks must be taken and prices paid if harmony is to be established as God wills it. He knows that consequences for which we are accountable flow from our decisions. In making such affirmations he is not churchy or spiritual but simply discerns that God's will and rule must be taken seriously and that, of course, is the ministry of the church.

Such a model for ministry requires quite different objectives and more modest expectations. Such a minister is not the enthusiastic reformer, crusader, or protester, but the reflector content to address specific issues and hope for change there. Such modest expectations prevent the kinds of frustrations which are sure to come if great results are expected and if great authority and influence are imagined which simply do not exist.

This model also requires a set of competences different from the conventional. It makes no less important a thorough grounding in biblical and theological disciplines, and it does not criticize the practice of preaching, counseling, etc. It does require skills appropriate to a ministry of reflection and consultation not usually central in a ministerial repertoire. These include skill in program and resource development, conflict management, process management, and such related competences that have no narrow, peculiar "religious" concern, though they are not without a theological dimension. Such a form and conception of ministry corresponds to the suggestion of H. R. Niebuhr of the minister as "director," i.e., one who operates with managerial skills to mobilize resources with reference to human priorities.

Such a ministry is surely at the margin of what we have usually conceived of as ministry. It minimizes the visible sacral apparatus. It leaves one without conventional identity, support, or job description.

But conventional ministry models are also increasingly marginal. The action is not only at the altar or in the pulpit, but also in the laboratory, in the meetings of corporate boards, and in the chancellor's office.

The wise in Israel were at the matrix of real power but at the margin of structural authority. They had great influence but not much official position. They stood close to the king, were not much noticed on high holy days, but they bent public policy. As we pursue this new emphasis in Scripture study in relation to ministry we may discover that matrix is really margin and margin is increasingly matrix.

Ministry at the matrix in any visible way belongs to a situation in which persons are dependent upon the church and its ministry for meaning and guidance. Such a ministry belongs to a sacrally ordered society, which in our time is gone. Whether we like it or not, we are being pressed to and permitted maturity. We may not like it and we may resist it. We may botch it. But toward maturity is where we are going.

Ministry is no less important, but it must be a ministry which takes full account of its own maturity, of the maturity of those with whom it has to do and most especially with the God who calls us to maturity. That ministry is shown to us in the ministry of Jesus of Nazareth, who called both obedient servants out of their bondage and abandoned orphans back to their father. His actions and teachings called persons and society to maturity and enabled them to embrace it.

VII.
Uneasy Reflections from a Son of Neoorthodoxy

The wisdom traditions are the voice of protest which must always remain a minority voice, which is not dazzled by the prepared answer, and which is not so impressed with business as usual that it thinks this is the only way to do business. The wisdom teachers are keenly aware of the self-deception which tempts us in all our learning and not least in theology. They serve to keep us honest, occasionally to call a halt to our self-confident charade. From time to time they ask us if we are for real.

Sometimes we are not for real. Faith can become a way to work the system, to explain life, and to manipulate for our own ends. Theology can also become safe and respectable so that it is the announcement of yesterday's authenticities in the face of new realities, the parroting of old certainties, the defense of old positions, the insistence upon old questions, the passion to make events and persons fit the scheme of how they are supposed to be.

Wisdom is a surprising resource for the continual reexamination of Israel's faith. The wise man in his method sought to be always in dialogue with the reality of his environment. He was always curious about the intricacies of his social order, the delicacy of human relationship, the marvel and mystery of his natural environment. He always wanted to know. He would not settle for yesterday's answers but asked how it looks today.

Proverbs, of course, is an example of a style of life in which men really ask about the message given in their environment. In such a dialogue nothing is trivial or safely ignored. Each small turn of events speaks a word to us and discloses a freshness about the world in which we live. The word spoken is often a new word, unexpected, not in conformity with how we thought it should be and always was.

Proverbs thus embodies an approach to life of disciplined curiosity which we may call "scientific": wanting to know about the world in which we live and the resources available to us. The method of such inquiry, when properly done, involves waiting for new disclosures, being attentive and responsible to them, and receiving them when they come, even if it means the abandonment of what was precious and had seemed true.

In a more powerful way Job also shows that faith is a dialogue with one's world, that doing theology is maintaining intellectual discipline and honesty. Thus the poet's method in the book of Job permits him to cut through the phoniness of his contemporaries. He recognizes that they were not really in dialogue with their world but only with their private, professional, selected data about the world. If one selects carefully enough then the data fits the scheme and we can think things are settled. But the poet insists that we must face all the data. This includes a strange stillness in the cosmos when one expects a word. It includes virtue unrewarded and morality unrecognized. These are data that do not fit the scheme but they are there. The poet sees that the first step in any real faith or significant theology is to affirm that life is really like that.

That, as I see it, is the primary value of our recovery of the wisdom traditions in our handling of Scripture. Dialogue should not be so threatening, but it often is. It is radical to say that all the questions must be faced again and again in light of the data, but that is precisely the radicalness of the wise teachers. They had the shrewdness to see the dangers of a monarchal establishment concerned only about itself, so they warn against pride (Prov. 11:2; 13:10; 29:23). The Proverbs tell it like it is. They resist the notion of the received tradition that God will do it for us, and not so often recognized but pertinent to both the tenth century and our time, they warn against an aggressive self-assertion when responsibility becomes arrogance. Senator William J. Fulbright in his book *The Arrogance of Power* has functioned as a wise man in our government.

It is curious yet understandable that wisdom traditions have their greatest appeal with persons who do not think of themselves in terms of the establishment and traditions of orthodoxy. Many people in the church who are not accustomed to think of either faith or theology in terms of dialogue with the world around us find the new emphasis upon the wisdom traditions threatening. (To be sure, many others find it liberating, but it is wisdom as threat which I consider here.) To such a mood, all the radical movements of theology which we have mentioned in Chapter V appear to be threats, and no less so, wisdom.

Because such a theological effort is perceived as threat several possible approaches may be taken to portray the wisdom tradition as an illegitimate kind of theology.

One may ask if the wisdom tradition is *Scriptural.* This is an important question for those who hold that theology must in any case be rooted in the witness of Scripture. On the face of it, the motifs of wisdom theology which we have presented do not fit with our usual assumptions concerning Scripture. They don't fit into our usual formulations of salvation history, or the mighty acts of God, or any of the other dimensions of Mosaic-prophetic faith which are central in most church traditions.

The whole idea of a canon within the canon has assumed that the center of Scripture is to be found, for example, in Paul's teaching, in Romans, of justification by grace through faith. When that is perceived as the core of the Bible then obviously wisdom is only remotely related to the true subject of the Bible. So one may indeed dismiss wisdom as not biblical in the sense that idea is usually understood among the faithful.

Perhaps rather than to dismiss wisdom as non-biblical we ought to take a fresh look at what the Bible is really about. The first point is the recognition that wisdom is there in the Bible. For all of our disregard of it, it will not simply go away. We will have to deal with wisdom as an authentic part of Scripture even if it does not adjust to our preconceptions. This way of putting it suggests that it is not the wisdom traditions which are in question but our unfair, one-sided handling of Scripture: we have celebrated and used only those parts of Scripture which have supported our dogmatic presuppositions and commitments.

The radicalness of wisdom parts of Scripture is uncomfortable for us when we have made peace with the other parts, but we must face it. The radicalness of Proverbs is that we honor God by celebrating man and not debasing him. The radicalness of Job is that God is known in his awful holiness and his devastating absence which refutes our best attempts to maintain his presence on our own terms. Wisdom threatens our usual theological stance but is nonetheless Scriptural. For that reason its rediscovery is all the more urgent for us. If we hear this voice in the biblical tradition, we are driven to a new notion of the central witness of Scripture and perhaps to a reformulation of our canon within the canon.

A second question which can be asked in an attempt to discredit wisdom as a legitimate way of doing theology is this: *is wisdom theology faithful to our understanding of God?* On the face of it the answer could be in the affirmative. Proverbs talks about the "fear of Yahweh" and maintains for him the prerogative of the ultimate disposal of issues (Prov. 16:2, 9; 19:21; 20:24; 21:2, 30–31). Yet Proverbs is most often understood as humanistic, rationalistic, and utilitarian. It seems to suggest that if men are smart and quick enough life can be manipulated no matter what the purposes of God might be. This is also found in Job: though the voice on the whirlwind is decisive it is a hidden God with whom we feel less than comfortable. He seems rather uninvolved, and in any case he is scarcely the kind of God around which an institution can be formed.

Though these traditions speak of God they are a considerable threat to those who think they have come to terms with the God of the church. Their affirmations sound strange to the ears of a believer. The defensiveness in the church today against radical theology is not because of the transition in God-talk. Rather, offense is taken at the man-talk which wisdom nurtures. The man of Proverbs is not the servile, self-abasing figure often urged by our one-sided reading of Scripture in later Augustinian-Lutheran theological traditions. Rather he is an able, self-reliant, caring, involved, strong person who has a significant influence over the course of his own life and over the lives of his fellows. This kind of man-talk of course has implications for God-talk. Proverbs is not atheism, humanism, or secularism. It does not speak of the death of God but it has no patience for a god who only saves sinners and judges sins. The God affirmed here trusts man, believes in him, risks his world with him, and stays with him in his failures. The man envisioned by Proverbs is not a cosmic orphan nor a protected baby but a beloved son in a joyous home:

> . . . the LORD reproves him whom he loves, as a
> father the son in whom he delights. (Prov. 3:12)

The issue before us as we feel anxious about our theology going down the drain is not that wisdom could destroy theology or expose the whole enterprise of theology as a fraud. Rather, it exposes bad theology and calls us to unlearn wrong theology. It maintains a firm critique against a theology rooted in self-hatred, low self-esteem, weakness, misery, and despair. Thus perhaps wisdom theology is rightly perceived as threat, not because it denies God but because it calls us to unlearn our theology, to abandon a precarious vision which has lived in a small world now torn open.

The major affirmations of classical theology still hold in wisdom theology. I take those to be the sovereignty of God and the graciousness of God. But in this theology they must be redefined in radical ways. Wisdom affirms the sovereignty of God, but it is not a sovereignty which manages, determines, nags, and keeps books. The lordship of this God is witnessed in his relaxed delight, in his confidence about the well-being of the world, in the buoyancy to give his creatures considerable latitude because he has no anxiety or concern about the general direction of the emergence of life and heatlh in his world.

Sovereignty in much theology has been angry or at least grudging, but not so the theology of the wisdom men. They affirm a kind of lordship which has come to terms with the realm. They see lordship over a realm which acknowledges that lordship; which is not always in rebellion; which does not find lordship a burden but a meaningful context in which to live.

If this redefinition appears as a threat, then it should be clear that the affirmation of sovereignty is not what is in question. Rather, what is in question is the style of sovereignty—a fearful, suspicious, defensive lordship which can't believe in its own legitimacy. The sovereignty of God affirmed in wisdom is that of a God who accepts the legitimacy of his rule and therefore the legitimacy of the freedom of his human subjects. From such sovereignty much of the anxiety has disappeared, for affirmation permits one to feel quite differently about the world in which one must live.

The same is true of the motif of the graciousness of God. What is under criticism by a theology of wisdom is not whether God is gracious but what graciousness means. What is rejected is an understanding of graciousness as a maudlin supportiveness which is unquestioning and undemanding and is available any time we feel the need to cop out. Such a view of graciousness, fostered by the church, assumes that God's business concerns our weakness, failure, and misery. Conversely, as Bonhoeffer has said so clearly, men in their strength, success, and well-being have no need for such a God.

The graciousness of God as understood in wisdom is the kind a father feels toward a son whom he expects to mature and become an adult. It is graciousness which always stands by but which chastens, which always affirms but which never excuses carelessness or phoniness. It is graciousness which says "grow up." This graciousness addresses men in their strength, success, and well-being. It is not for the gaps but for a healthy identity in all our varying states.

The God of the wisdom tradition is firmly sovereign and consistently gracious, but his sovereignty never becomes petty, nor does his graciousness become sentimental. His sovereignty always gives men their due. His graciousness calls us to accountability. When wisdom theology threatens, it is not because the classical elements in our faith are under attack but because we have grown comfortable with perversions. Characteristically, this theology means for us to face those perversions and abandon them.

A third question which may be asked in an attempt to discredit wisdom theology as a legitimate way to do theology is: *doesn't such a faith make Jesus Christ unimportant if not dispensable?* That question of course occurs whenever Old Testament data becomes the key to our theological self-understanding, but the problem is even more acute with wisdom. Again, we must affirm that it is not Jesus Christ who is being called into question, but our distorted understanding of who he is.

The theology of the wisdom teachers which we have tried to exposit is consistent with the major thrust of Jesus' teaching. The Kingdom of God is, he proclaimed, a realm of wholeness, freedom, responsibility, and security where men can be the men God intends them to be. Indeed, to affirm that we do live in that kind of world is a close approximation of the world in which the wise said we lived. Jesus' teaching, particularly in Matthew, has remarkable confidence in man's capacity to be free, safe, whole, and responsible. He affirms that men are responsible for the future they choose (cf. Matt. 25: 31–46). He celebrates man as one who is especially precious and loved (Matt. 6:25–33). His teaching has the same buoyancy, confidence, and openness as that which characterizes wisdom teaching at its best.

The question is more pressing when we ask in conventional terms about the person and work of Jesus Christ, i.e., incarnation and atonement. Jesus embodies both what we most celebrate in the person of God and the teaching of the wise men about how one lives as a life-bringer. To speak of Jesus in terms of atonement of course stacks the cards in terms of man's helplessness and need. But insofar as Jesus does make a difference in the lives of persons, it is to invite them to join in his style of manhood, which is life-affirming and life-creating. He does not ponder long the failure of man but invites him to change and act as a whole healthy person. He embodies what the wise men said was possible.

Jesus Christ is then the manifestation in a human life of the kind of style the wise urged upon people. He also enables people to attain that style. By his presence men were able to leave off the ways of "folly" and embrace the ways of "wisdom" (cf. Matt. 25:1–13). Jesus of Nazareth may be the culmination of other traditions but he is no less the culmination of the wisdom tradition. In him we know clearly and unmistakably what it means to live as a wise one. Because he lived that way, we say our situation has been decisively changed.

This way of coming at Jesus in no way detracts from his central-ity, but it does call us to reexamine our ways of believing about him—ways which make of him a crutch, a rainmaker, and a medicine man. Rather, he is truly man, the kind which the wisdom tradition (Gen. 1:27–31) said God has always intended. Rather than attack this theology as a threat which must be discredited we would do well to learn from it, to listen to it and be changed by it.

Finally, one may seek to discredit this theology as a legitimate approach to our theological task by asking *if it is realistic.* It seems to be optimistic about man. It credits him with too much and does not take seriously our traditional affirmation about the fallenness and depravity of man.

In response we can make three affirmations which may illumi-nate the problem. First, Jesus himself had an incredibly confident approach to human personality. He clearly believed that persons could choose and live responsibly healthy lives. He had high expecta-tions toward those with whom he had to deal. Indeed, the whole notion of the depravity of man seems to be informed by a cultural situation much different from that of Jesus. In that regard the Jewish tradition has kept alive an important protest against the Christian emphasis upon the sinfulness and fallenness of man.

Second, much current research into human nature and human behavior (e.g. the work of Abraham Maslow), indicates that we live up to or down to our expectations. Set in situations in which health and maturity are expected of us we live toward them in amazing ways. The capacities of the human person to live and act in adult ways is almost untapped. It will not do any longer simply to say that we are "fallen" and cannot choose good but depend upon someone to give us health. Such an opinion does not square with the evidence at hand.

Third, with the tremendous power and knowledge now at our disposal, we need to think of ourselves in the most adult terms possible. It is risky business to foster a theology of inadequacy, incapability, and irresponsibility in a world where the stakes are so high and our power is so great. Because the Gospel promises precisely the persons needed in our technological world—namely adults—it makes no sense to see ourselves and our fellows in terms of our crippledness. If that continues to be the way we see ourselves, then we shall have played a major role in creating a context in which our knowledge and power get used in destructive ways. The fact of the matter is we are accountable and responsible. Our choices do matter and we do have real choices open to us.

If we are to be realistic about our human potential we are compelled to say realistically that we are responsible. We can decide for life or death. No God anywhere will bail us out. Realism does not mean simply to repeat a theological tradition but to look at our actual situation. It is realism to say that only adults can cope with our present situation. It is sheer obscurantism to say that we are incapable or incompetent, because in our precarious world we really have no options but to live up to the style urged by the wisdom teachers and to which we are summoned by Jesus Christ.

Thus we can affirm that wisdom theology is:

> Biblical: much of Scripture makes the affirmations of man we have attributed to wisdom.

> Faithful to our understanding of God: it affirms his sovereignty and his graciousness but not at the expense of maturing man.

> Responsible in terms of the role of Jesus Christ: who embodies the man wisdom anticipates and summons others to their full manhood.

> Realistic: it recognizes the real situation and the real resources available to us.

For us it can perform in a most important way its function as critic. It can force us to reexamine and unlearn and learn anew.

Before I stop I add a word of uneasiness, not because it voids the argument presented above nor because my own uneasiness is of interest in the discussion, but because such uneasiness is, I believe, an integral part of this theological revolution for persons in my generation. I state it here to invite people to the company of the uneasy and to acknowledge that the theological turn-around implicit in the argument is a difficult one which cannot be made easily by some without a troubled conscience. The uneasiness has to do with what we are to make of our theological nurture and heritage. To me, and I think to many others, it is in fact a direct development of our heritage, but we are not quite sure. There lies the uneasiness or so it seems to a son of neoorthodoxy.

The uneasiness about the relation of the turnaround to our heritage has many facets. Is it faithful to the sixteenth-century reformation and the massive rebirth of faith to which we are heirs? It has been my intention throughout the present discussion to take with utmost seriousness the great Reformation themes of divine sovereignty and graciousness as the way of justification. Rather than deny these great themes, the affirmations I have made seek to reassert what has been neglected in a one-sided memory of the Reformation. The Lordship of God has tended to overwhelm the theme of vocation and the Reformation emphasis upon human responsibility. Only perverted Reformation theology of justification has resulted in "cheap grace." I understand my argument in light of the Reformation and its primary affirmations.

My uneasiness also is linked to the suggestion that this theology is not really informed by the biblical tradition, but is an accommodation to current fads in the behavioral sciences. The suggestion is double-pronged and I can only express my uneasiness and give no answer beyond those already suggested. I regard it as profoundly biblical. This theology is not a departure from the tradition of Scripture but a reassertion of what we have neglected in making Scripture serve our theological investments. The charge that this theology accommodates secular learning raises very difficult hermeneutical questions. Consistent with the wise men of Israel, this theology would affirm that insight comes from all sorts of sources including the secular disciplines of learning. That insight comes from such a source in no way discredits it. Our task is not to hold for biblical truths in isolation from all other learnings, but rather to bring all our other insights to bear upon our illumination of Scripture. Obviously, this response will not satisfy some because it is made out of different hermeneutical presuppositions from those which prompt the charge. In a way this issue is really the point of the whole thing, and additional words won't change that.

Finally, it may be asked if this isn't really a return to the "social Gospel" of the nineteenth century. Such a "social Gospel" is often discredited now, and where it is held it is an embarrassment. In answer I would suggest that hopefully we are more sober and realistic, not romantic about our chances of changing the world. I also think it appropriate and positive to link this theology to the older social Gospel, for that theology affirmed correctly that any salvation is to be found in the shape of the secular community and through the efforts of persons in that community. Like every significant theology it is one-sided in making some points and neglecting others, but like the social Gospel, for our time it makes the right points and neglects the ones that need to be neglected.

My uneasiness is really rooted in my self-understanding. I find myself doing a kind of theology which I do not expect myself to be doing. Each time it surprises me because it is in some ways a radical departure from all that I have been taught and think I believe. If I were more pious I would say I have been unable to resist the guidance of the Holy Spirit. I prefer to say I have been pressed by the times. In that context my Scripture studies lead me this way and it makes sense in light of our times as I understand it. Moreover, it makes sense to the people whose judgment about sense and nonsense I trust and respect.

No doubt being pressed in this way and led to these conclusions is largely determined by my autobiography, as is the case of most of the people engaged with the turnaround in theology. The same is true of every theology, and perhaps it is really the autobiography of our generation. From that it may follow that it is only a tract for the time, perhaps a very brief time, but just now it is a tract that should be offered. Perhaps in a short time its moment will be past, although there are strong hints that we can never go back home again. The times promise that and our Scripture also asserts it, because we are followers of "the Way," which goes only one way.

So I end with the uneasiness I have lived with in formulating this study. I regard it as faithful to the core of the faith of my fathers and something that I want to say clearly and passionately to my sons. I end with uneasiness about the whole effort, but that is the way theology must always be done. That is something the wise men never doubted.

Abbreviations Used in Notes and Appendix

Notes

I. Religious Despisers of Culture

1. This title was suggested by my colleague, Ernest Nolte. It will be recognized as an inversion of the problem addressed by Schleiermacher in *On Religion, Addresses in Response to Its Cultured Critics* (Richmond: John Knox Press, 1969).
2. I have suggested some aspects of this problem in "The Triumphalist Tendency in Exegetical History," JAAR, Vol. XXXVIII (December 1970), pp. 367–380.
3. "The Kerygma of the Book of Proverbs," *Interpretation*, Vol. XX (January 1966), pp. 3–14.
4. Tr. by John A. Wilson in *Ancient Near Eastern Texts Relating to the Old Testament*, ed. James Pritchard (2nd ed.; Princeton: Princeton University Press, 1955), pp. 421–425.
5. Robert Theobald, "Freedom in Education," *Journal of Higher Education* (Pub. by The United Church of Christ; April 1969), p. 14, makes a most helpful distinction between "structural authority" and "sapiential authority." Walter J. Harrelson, "Wisdom and Pastoral Theology," *Andover-Newton Quarterly*, Vol. VII (September 1966), pp. 6–14, has observed that Ann Landers continues the tradition of the wise teacher. She simply tells how it is without claim to any office or authority. When she is occasionally challenged by her readers, she responds, "Perhaps it is not like that, if your experience teaches otherwise."
6. Von Rad, *Old Testament Theology*, I (New York: Harper & Row, 1962), p. 439, has noted a series of passages from Proverbs which affirms Yahweh's inscrutable freedom in the face of human choices. See a more recent discussion in von Rad's *Weisheit in Israel* (Neukirchen-Vluyn: Neukirchener Verlag, 1970), pp. 131ff., and W. Zimmerli, "The Place and Limit of the Wisdom in the Framework of the Old Testament Theology," SJT, Vol. XVII (1964), p. 158. In a different context, cf. G. D. Kaufman, "On the Meaning of 'God': Transcendence Without Mythology," HTR, Vol. LIX (April 1966), pp. 105–132.
7. The importance of trust in personhood has been especially stressed by Carl Rogers, *On Becoming a Person*, and Erik Erikson, *Childhood and Society*. Rogers has been concerned with combating the dominant negative view of man in theology generally, and Erikson has been concerned with basic human trust as an essential factor in the building of viable community.
8. The term is used by John Knowles in *A Separate Peace*, probably borrowed from Hemingway's *A Farewell to Arms*. It represents an attempt to create a private sphere of well-being apart from the larger community and is closely related to coveting, so roundly condemned in wisdom (cf. Prov. 21:26; 28:16; Luke 12:22–34; Acts 5:1–11). Our cultural scene witnesses many attempts at a separate peace.
9. Among the discussions of theology and environmental responsibility, cf. Richard L. Means, "Man and Nature: The Theological Vacuum," *Christian Century* (May 1, 1968), pp. 579–581; "Why Worry About Nature?" *Saturday Review* (December 2, 1967), pp. 13–15; Lynn White, Jr., "The Historical Roots of Our Ecologic Crisis," *Science* (March 10, 1967), pp. 1203–1207; and my article, "King in the

Kingdom of Things," *Christian Century* (September 10, 1969), pp. 1165–1166.

10. Walther Zimmerli, "The Place and Limit of the Wisdom in the Framework of the Old Testament Theology," *op. cit.*, p. 148.

11. This motif is stressed in the work of F. Gogarten, "Theology and History," *History and Hermeneutic*, JTC, Vol. IV, pp. 35–81. Cf. also, Larry E. Shiner, *The Secularization of History* (Nashville: Abingdon Press, 1966). Gunther Bornkamm, *Jesus of Nazareth* (New York: Harper & Row, 1961), pp. 87ff., speaks about Jesus' teaching in a way that is very parallel to that of a wisdom teacher.

II. The Trusted Creature

1. Cf. von Rad, "The Beginnings of Historical Writing in Ancient Israel," *The Problem of the Hexateuch and Other Essays* (New York: McGraw-Hill Book Co., 1966), pp. 176ff.

2. On the role of Samuel as covenant mediator, cf. R. Rendtorff, "Reflections on the Early History of Prophecy in Israel," *History and Hermeneutic*, JTC, Vol. IV, pp. 14–34; Hans-Joachim Kraus, *Die prophetische Verkündigung des Rechts in Israel*, pp. 23ff.; James Muilenburg, "Covenantal Formulations," VT, Vol. IX (1959), pp. 347–365. On the emergence of the monarchy, cf. J. A. Soggin, "Zur Entwicklung des alttestamentlichen Königtums," TZ, Vol. XV (1959), pp. 401–418, and "Charisma und Institution im Königtum Sauls," ZAW, Vol. LXXV (1963), pp. 54–65.

3. Among the many discussions of the questions, cf. Rost, "Davidsbund und Sinaibund," TLZ, Vol. LXXII (1947), cols. 129–134; Ronald E. Clements, *Abraham and David* (Naperville, Ill.: Alec R. Allenson, 1967), pp. 79ff.; Murray L. Newman, *The People of the Covenant* (Nashville: Abingdon Press, 1962).

4. Cf. von Rad *Old Testament Theology*, I, pp. 36ff., and Walter Harrelson, "Prophecy and Syncretism," *Andover-Newton Quarterly*, Vol. IV (March 1964), pp. 6–19, on the possible positive dimensions of syncretism.

5. The shepherd boy motif is ambiguous, because on the one hand it describes one without any claims at all, but on the other hand the shepherd motif is closely related to kingship (cf. 2 Samuel 5:2, and the discussion of Hans Gottlieb, "Die Tradition von David als Hirten," VT, Vol. XVII (1967), pp. 190–200.

6. As Gerstenberger and Richter have shown, wisdom is much older. Here I mean simply that it became an important intellectual option for Israel only because of the new cultural situation created by David. While the actual appearance of wisdom is credited to Solomon, David's achievements both required and permitted it.

7. I have argued that "man" in Genesis 2 from the tenth century refers to the royal man—the king; cf. "David and His Theologian," CBQ, Vol. XXX (1968), pp. 156–181. The later creation story in Genesis 1 certainly ascribes the royal place to the man created there; cf. Bernhard W. Anderson, *Creation vs. Chaos* (New York: Association Press, 1967), p. 177.

8. "Zur Struktur der alttestamentlichen Weisheit," ZAW, Vol. XLV (1933), pp. 194ff.

9. The king, as in the case of David, is especially responsible for "life." Cf. Sigmund Mowinckel, *He That Cometh* (Nashville: Abingdon Press, 1956), pp. 89ff., and Aubrey Johnson, *Sacral Kingship in Ancient Israel* (Cardiff: University of Wales Press, 1955), and Johannes Pederson, *Israel* (New York: Oxford University Press, 1926), pp. 81–85.

III. Theology Fit for a King

1. See the summary of historical and archeological data by William F. Albright, *Archaeology and the Religion of Israel* (Baltimore: Johns Hopkins Press, 1956), pp. 130–155. On the theological crisis of the period, cf. von Rad, *Old Testament Theology,* I, pp. 36–38.

2. Von Rad, *ibid.,* pp. 48–56. In his more recent *Weisheit in Israel,* pp. 82ff., 132ff., 239ff., the theme of tenth-century "Enlightenment" is pervasive. Cf. Roger N. Whybray, *The Succession Narrative,* Studies in Biblical Theology, 2nd Series, No. 9 (Naperville, Ill.: Alec R. Allenson, 1968), p. 4.

3. On the dating, the work of Albright, "Some Canaanite-Phoenician Sources of Hebrew Wisdom," VTS, Vol. III (1955), pp. 1–15, is important. Cf. also C. Kayatz, *Studien zu Proverbien,* WMANT, 28 (Neukirchen-Vluyn: Neukirchener Verlag, 1966). The work of Gerstenberger and Richter also tends to argue for an early date. There are, of course, various collections in Proverbs from various times; certainly not all of these are early. But even in Proverbs 1—9, commonly thought to be later, there can be little doubt that older materials have been utilized. Thus, in arguing for the tenth century as a context for wisdom I do not refer to any specific document, but to the stock of wisdom teaching contained in the materials we now possess.
   It is not necessary to date them as late as does R. B. Y. Scott in "Solomon and the Beginnings of Wisdom in Israel," SVT, Vol. III (1955), pp. 262–279. Cf. also M. Noth, "Die Bewährung von Solomos 'Gottlicher Weisheit,' " *ibid.,* pp. 225–237.

4. Von Rad, *Old Testament Theology,* I, p. 439, has listed some important passages, but his more recent study, *Weisheit in Israel,* focuses much more extensively on the same issue.

5. Von Rad, "The Beginnings of Historical Writing in Ancient Israel," *The Problem of the Hexateuch and Other Essays,* pp. 176–204, and R. N. Whybray, *The Succession Narrative, op. cit.*

6. Von Rad, *ibid.,* p. 198, has especially stressed the three passages in 2 Samuel 11:27; 12:24; 17:14. For the staying power of the promise against the choices of the royal family, cf. my discussion in "David and His Theologian," *op. cit.,* pp. 175ff.

7. It is now generally accepted that this earliest stratum of the Pentateuch is from the tenth century and does its theologizing with reference to the monarchy. While we here focus on the prehistory, another fruitful line of investigation would be the Joseph Narrative. On the Yahwist, cf. especially von Rad, *Old Testament Theology,* I, pp. 161–165, and H. W. Wolff, "The Kerygma of the Yahwist," *Interpretation,* Vol. XX (April 1966), pp. 131–158, to which the reference is here made.

8. "David and His Theologian," *op. cit.,* pp. 156–181.

9. Of particular importance are the papers by J. Blenkinsopp, "Theme and Motif in the Succession History (2 Sam. 11:2ff.) and the Yahwist Corpus," VTS, Vol. XV (1966), pp. 44–57. and Alonso-Schoekel, "Sapiential and Covenant Themes in Genesis 2—3," *Modern Biblical Studies,* ed. D. J. McCarthy and W. B. Callen (Milwaukee: Bruce Pub. Co., 1967), pp. 49–61.

10. Cf. Thomas W. Ogletree, "From Anxiety to Responsibility: The Shifting Focus of Theological Reflection," *New Theology No. 6,* ed. Martin E. Marty and Dean G. Peerman (New York: Macmillan Co., 1969), pp. 35–65. Ogletree is not interested in the biblical data as such, but indicates fresh directions for biblical study.

IV. Tempted to Commodities

1. I am using the word "things" after the manner of C. Bonifazi, *A Theology of Things* (Philadelphia: Lippincott, 1967).
2. Joseph Haas and Gene Lovitz, *Carl Sandburg, A Pictorial Biography* (New York: G. P. Putnam's Sons, 1967), pp. 14–16.
3. Harvey Cox, *The Secular City* (New York: Macmillan), 1966; A. Van Leeuwen, *Christianity in World History* (London: Edinburgh House Press, 1964).
4. In his more recent book, *The Feast of Fools* (Cambridge: Harvard University Press, 1969), he has more fully faced our Western problem. This book appears to be a corrective to the one-sided appreciation of the secular-technological in his earlier writing. Other efforts in the same direction include Sam Keen, *Apology for Wonder* (New York: Harper & Row, 1969), *To a Dancing God* (New York: Harper & Row, 1970), and Robert E. Neale, *In Praise of Play* (New York: Harper & Row, 1969).
5. Van Leeuwen's more recent book, *Prophecy in a Technocratic Era* (New York: Charles Scribner's Sons, 1968), more directly addresses these questions.
6. Abraham J. Heschel *Who is Man?* (Stanford, Calif.: Stanford University Press, 1965), pp. 82–83.
7. I have been helped most by the suggestions of Gogarten and his stress on the slave-son theme in Galatians 4:1–7. Cf. the summary and review by L. Shiner, *The Secularization of History*.
8. Perhaps Ralph Nader is presently our most eloquent reminder that the world is not primarily a commodity.

V. The Meaning of Maturity for Current Theology

1. Harvey Cox, *The Secular City* (New York: Macmillan Co., 1966), p. 1.
2. Arend van Leeuwen, *Christianity in World History* (London: Edinburgh House Press, 1965).
3. H. Richard Niebuhr, *Radical Monotheism and Western Culture* (New York: Harper & Row, 1970), p. 52.
4. For an English summary of Gogarten's work, cf. L. Shiner, *The Secularization of History*.
5. A very useful summary of the nuances in retribution theology is provided by John Gammie, "The Theology of Retribution in the Book of Deuteronomy," CBQ, Vol. XXXII (1970), pp. 1–12.
6. Von Rad, *Weisheit in Israel*, p. 129. Moshe Weinfeld, "Deuteronomy—The Present State of Inquiry," JBL, Vol. LXXXVI (1967), pp. 249–262, has been helpful on secularization in Israel's tradition.
7. Joseph Fletcher, *Situation Ethics: The New Morality* (Philadelphia: Westminster Press, 1966). Joseph Fletcher, *Moral Responsibility: Situation Ethics at Work* (Philadelphia: Westminster Press, 1967).
8. E. Gerstenberger, *Wesen und Herkunft des "apodiktischen Rechts"* (Neukirchen-Vluyn: Neukirchener Verlag, 1965). See the summary in English in J. J. Stamm and M. E. Andrew, *The Ten Commandments in Recent Research*, Studies in Biblical Theology, 2nd Series, No. 2 (London: S.C.M. Press, 1967), p. 38–51.
9. "A Different 2001," *Journal of Higher Education* (Published by The United Church of Christ; Jan.–Feb. 1970), pp. 10–14.
10. "See Everything, Do Everything, Feel Nothing," *Saturday Review* (Jan. 23, 1971), p. 31.

11. *Weisheit in Israel,* pp. 306–308.
12. Possible meanings of the formula have been summarized by William Hamilton and Thomas J. Altizer, *Radical Theology and the Death of God* (New York: Bobbs-Merrill, 1966), pp. x–xi. In addition to those essays, the basic literature on the topic includes: Paul Van Buren, *The Secular Meaning of the Gospel* (New York: Macmillan Co., 1963); Thomas J. Altizer, *The Gospel of Christian Atheism* (Philadelphia: Westminster Press, 1966) and *Toward a New Christianity: Readings in the Death of God Theology* (New York: Harcourt, Brace and World, 1967); William Hamilton, *The New Essence of Christianity* (New York: Association Press, 1961); Gabriel Vahanian, *Wait Without Idols* (New York: G. Braziller, 1964); Richard L. Rubenstein, *After Auschwitz; Radical Theology and Contemporary Judaism* (Indianapolis: Bobbs-Merrill, 1966) and *The Religious Imagination: A Study in Psychoanalysis and Jewish Theology* (Boston: Beacon Press, 1968). In response to these, cf. Langdon Gilkey, *Naming the Whirlwind: The Renewal of God-Language* (New York: Bobbs-Merrill, 1969).
13. Von Rad, *Weisheit in Israel,* pp. 82ff., 131ff.
14. *The Religious Imagination,* pp. xviiif., and more extensively in "Job and Auschwitz," USQR, Vol. XXV (1969–70), pp. 421–437.
15. Cf. James H. Smylie, "On Jesus, Pharaohs, and the Chosen People," *Interpretation,* Vol. XXIV (January 1970), pp. 74–91.
16. This image has been explored by Jerry Farber, "The Student as Nigger," *The Student as Nigger* (New York: Pocket Books, 1970), pp. 114–128.
17. My summary statement is found in "Scripture and an Ecumenical Life-Style," *Interpretation,* Vol. XXIV (January 1970), pp. 3–10.

VI. The Wise Man as a Model for Ministry

1. Cf. Gerald J. Jud, Edgar W. Mills, Jr., and Genevieve W. Burch, *Ex-Pastors: Why Men Leave the Parish Ministry* (Philadelphia: Pilgrim Press, 1970).
2. Kenneth Underwood *et al., The Church, the University, and Social Policy* (Middletown, Conn.: Wesleyan University Press, 1969).
3. The point is made in several of his writings. Cf. *Das amt des propheten bei Amos,* FRLANT, 80 (Göttiugen: Vandenhoeck and Ruprecht, 1962); *Liturgie und prophetisches Ich bei Jeremia* (Gütersloher Verlaghaus, 1963); and *Wächter über Israel; Ezechiel und seine Tradition,* BZAW, 82 (Berlin: A. Töpelmann, 1962).
4. Horst Symanowski, *The Christian Witness in an Industrial Society* (Philadelphia: Westminster Press, 1964), p. 50.
5. James Gustafson, "Towards Maturity in Decision-Making," *Christian Century* (July 10, 1968), pp. 894–898.
6. Robert W. Lynn, "A Ministry on the Margin," *The Church, the University, and Social Policy,* II, pp. 19–24, has suggested this language.

Appendix:
Recent Study in Wisdom Traditions

Because of the abundance of recent literature it is not possible to provide a complete bibliography. What follows presents some of the more important studies which have shaped current scholarly discussion.

Consideration of the contemporary discussion of wisdom may begin with Johannes Fichtner, *Die altorientalische weisheit in ihrer israelitisch-jüdischen Ausprägung* (Giessen: A Töpelmann, 1933). This book set forth the major motifs and themes of the wisdom literature. In the same year Walther Zimmerli, "Zur Struktur der alttestamentliche Weisheit," ZAW, Vol. LI (1933), pp. 177–204, focused more sharply on the urgent existential question of securing and understanding one's life. More recently Zimmerli, "The Place and Limit of the Wisdom in the Framework of the Old Testament Theology," SJT, Vol. XVII (1964), pp. 146–158, has asserted the relation between wisdom and creation theology. The work of Fichtner and Zimmerli are important because they take seriously the theological issues and questions which motivated the efforts of the wisdom traditions.

After a considerable gap in the discussion there has been a rapid increase in the literature. Several books in English have summarized the major ideas of wisdom and surveyed the various pieces of wisdom literature. These include J. C. Rylaarsdam, *Revelation in Jewish Wisdom Literature* (Chicago: University of Chicago Press, 1946) and Helmer Ringgren, *Word and Wisdom* (Lund: Ohlssons, 1947). Whereas Rylaarsdam considers a variety of theological themes in wisdom, Ringgren focuses on questions related to the hypostatization of wisdom in the ancient Near East. Both books are important because they are the primary contributions in the decade of World War II when new literature was not forthcoming.

The primary stimulus for the current discussion has been the influential work of Gerhard von Rad, *Old Testament Theology,* I (London: Oliver and Boyd, 1962), pp. 418–459. In this essay, which has dominated subsequent study, von Rad explored the theological thrust of wisdom in terms of coping with and ordering our common experience. In his most recent discussion, *Weisheit in Israel* (Neukirchen-Vluyn: Neukirchener Verlag, 1970), von Rad has expanded these themes with special attention to the "Enlightenment" period in Israel's history. He has also gone further in suggesting that wisdom represents for Israel an alternative theological option standing apart from the more familiar historical-prophetic traditions.

Following von Rad's early work came Harmut Gese's *Lehre und Wirklichkeit in der alten Weisheit* (Tübingen: J. C. B. Mohr, 1958), which gave special attention to the links between Israelite and Egyptian wisdom. Gese dealt carefully with the problem of grace in a theology of order. He found an important distinction here between the wisdom of Israel and her neighbors. Whereas Gese's book was concerned with a comparative study, U. Skladny, *Die ältesten Spruchsammlungen in Israel* (Göttingen: Vandenhoeck and Ruprecht, 1962), analyzed the major groupings of the early proverbs in Proverbs 10—21; 25—29, considering the major motifs which recur.

In more recent years, H. H. Schmidt, *Wesen und Geschichte der Weisheit*, BZAW, 101 (Berlin: A. Töpelmann, 1966), has explored the meaning and theology of Israel's wisdom in relation to that of Egypt and Mesopotamia. Returning to some of Gese's themes, though in larger scope, he deals with the question of the interaction between wisdom, cult, and myth. Schmidt is especially concerned with the links between wisdom and history. He observes an important development in wisdom as it interacts with historical pressures and influences.

At the same time, Erhard Gerstenberger, *Wesen und Herkunft des apodiktischen Rechts*, WMANT, 20 (Neukirchen-Vluyn: Neukirchener Verlag, 1965), and Wolfgang Richter, *Recht und Ethos*, SANT, 15, (München: Kösel-Verlag, 1966), consider the sapiential backgrounds of Israel's formulations. Of the two, Gerstenberger's book has exercised great influence on the study of the antiquity of wisdom and its relation to the various institutions in Israel's life. He has contended that one form for wisdom teaching emerged out of the domestic teaching of tribal wisdom. There is a summary in J. J. Stamm and M. E. Andrew, *The Ten Commandments in Recent Re-*

search, Studies in Biblical Theology, 2nd Series, No. 2 (London: S. C. M. Press, 1967). Gerstenberger thus made a major attack on an earlier consensus on law interpretation in ancient Israel.

Also concerned with origins, Hans-Jurgen Hermission, *Studien zur israelitischen Spruchweisheit,* WMANT, 28 (Neukirchen-Vluyn: Neukirchener Verlag, 1968), in a vigorous challenge to Gerstenberger has explored the role of wisdom schools in the origin and use of wisdom. A more specific study by C. Kayatz, *Studien zu Proverbien 1–9,* WMANT, 22 (Neukirchen-Vluyn: Neukirchener Verlag, 1966), has contributed to the tendency of earlier dating for wisdom by urging an earlier dating for the collection of Proverbs 1—9, usually thought to be the latest material in the book of Proverbs.

Finally among the major contributions, William McKane, *Proverbs* (Philadelphia: Westminster Press, 1970), has provided a massive and exhaustive summary of ancient Near Eastern wisdom in Egypt and Mesopotamia as an introduction to his commentary. He has also provided an extended discussion of literary forms as they relate to the Proverbs materials.

In addition to these larger studies which will influence subsequent work there has been a concern to locate wisdom influences in various parts of the Old Testament. Some of this work has been careless and ill-defined, but as a whole, these efforts have been suggestive in opening up new fields of investigation. The most important criticism of this effort is by J. L. Crenshaw, "Method in Determining Wisdom Influence Upon 'Historical' Writing," JBL, Vol. LXXXVIII (1969), pp. 129–142. He has rightly warned against a lack of clear definitions and methods which has resulted in doubtful investigations and questionable conclusions.

Among the valuable studies listed in the sequence of the canon are:

Genesis: Zimmerli's article, "The Place and Limit of the Wisdom in the Framework of the Old Testament Theology," has especially explored the meaning of wisdom for creation theology. This of course bears upon interpretation in Genesis 1—2. On the J prehistory, specific studies include those of J. Blenkinsopp, "Theme and Motif in the Succession History (2 Sam. 11:2ff.) and the Yahwist Corpus," VTS,

Vol. XV (1965), pp. 44–57, and Alonso-Schoekel, "Sapiential and Covenant Themes in Genesis 2—3," *Modern Biblical Studies,* ed. by D. S. McCarthy and William B. Callen (Milwaukee: Bruce Pub. Co., 1967), pp. 49–61. Von Rad's new book, *Weisheit in Israel,* has also given much attention to the relation between creation and wisdom, with the witness of creation as a countertheme to historical act in the study of revelation.

On the Joseph narrative, von Rad, "The Joseph Narrative and Ancient Wisdom," *The Problem of the Hexateuch and Other Essays* (New York: McGraw-Hill, 1966), pp. 292–300, has written an extremely influential essay, suggesting that Joseph is presented as a model man according to wisdom ideals. This essay has motivated similar proposals in other parts of Scripture.

Exodus. In addition to the works of Gerstenberger and Richter already mentioned dealing with the relation of wisdom and law, cf. Karl Elliger, "Das Gesetz Leviticus 18," ZAW, Vol. LXVII (1955), pp. 1–25. Though Elliger is not concerned with the precise question of wisdom, his essay has been an important one in understanding law in the context of tribal teaching and so supports Gerstenberger's general hypothesis. Robert Dentan, "The Literary Affinities of Exodus XXXIV 6f.," VT, Vol. XIII (1963), pp. 34–51, has attributed the formula of Exodus 34:6f. (which occurs nine times in the Old Testament in various forms) to wisdom theology which he contrasts with the theology of salvation history. This formula focuses upon the "attributes" of Yahweh rather than his acts.

Deuteronomy. The relation of Deuteronomy to wisdom has been widely explored and it is likely that this relationship is as well established as any which has been suggested. Cf. Moshe Weinfeld: "The Origin of Humanism in Deuteronomy," JBL, Vol. LXXX (1961), pp. 241–247; "The Dependence of Deuteronomy Upon Wisdom," *Kaufman Jubilee Volume* (1960), in Hebrew; "The Source of the Idea of Reward in Deuteronomy," *Tarbiz* (1960), pp. 8–15, in Hebrew; and "Deuteronomy—The Present State of Enquiry," JBL, Vol. LXXXVI (1967), pp. 249–262. There is also Jean Malfroy, "Sagesse et Loi dans le Deuteronome Etudes," VT, Vol. XV (1965), pp. 49–65.

Two Samuel. R. Norman Whybray, *The Succession Narrative,*

Studies in Biblical Theology; 2nd Series, No. 9 (London: S.C.M. Press, 1968), following von Rad, has argued that this literary achievement is informed by wisdom thought. Cf. also R. A. Carlson, *David the Chosen King,* (Uppsala: Almqvist and Wiksell, 1964), and Norman Porteous, "Royal Wisdom," VTS, Vol. III (1955), pp. 247–261.

Prophets. The relation between wisdom and prophecy is difficult but has been investigated by J. Lindblom, "Wisdom in the Old Testament Prophets," VTS, Vol. III (1955), pp. 192–204, and William McKane, *Prophets and Wisemen,* Studies in Biblical Theology 44 (Naperville Ill.: Alec R. Allenson, 1965). On specific prophets, the following two in particular have seemed likely candidates for a link with wisdom.

Isaiah. This relation was especially explored by Fichtner, "Jesaja unter den Weisen," *Gottes Weisheit* (Stuttgart: Calwer Verlag, 1965), pp. 18–26, and "Jahwes Plan in der Botschaft des Jesaja," *ibid.,* pp. 27–43. Cf. also Ilse von Loewenclau, "Zur Auslegung von Jesaja 1, 2—3," EvTh, 26 (1966), pp. 294–308. R. B. Y. Scott," Solomon and the Beginnings of Wisdom in Israel," VTS, Vol. III (1955), pp. 262–279, has proposed that the time of Isaiah was especially open to wisdom influences. Developing and reevaluating Fichtner's proposals, cf. most recently J. W. Whedbee, *Isaiah and Wisdom* (New York: Abingdon Press, 1971).

Amos. Samuel Terrien, "Amos and Wisdom," *Israel's Prophetic Heritage,* ed. B. Anderson and W. Harrelson (New York: Harper & Row, 1962), pp. 108–115, has suggested a connection between Amos and wisdom traditions and more recently, H. W. Wolff, *Amos' geistige heimat,* WMANT, 18 (Neukirchen-Vluyn: Neukirchener Verlag, 1965) has given the proposal his powerful support. For a review of this problem, cf. J. L. Crenshaw, "The Influence of the Wise upon Amos," ZAW, Vol. LXXIX (1967), pp. 42–52.

Of lesser importance for understanding wisdom at the moment, though suggestive for future work, are: James Muilenberg, who suggests a relation between Baruch and wisdom which would greatly alter our understanding of the Jeremiah tradition, and Donald E. Gowan, "Habakkuk and Wisdom," *Pittsburgh Perspectives,* Vol. IX (Summer 1968), pp. 157–166, who explores possible connections in Habukkuk.

Psalms. The questions involving the relation of wisdom and Psalms are many and complex, but see the summaries of Mowinckel, "Psalms and Wisdom," VTS, Vol. III (1955), pp. 205–224, and Roland Murphy, "A Consideration of the Classification 'Wisdom Psalms,'" VTS, Vol. IX (1962), pp. 156–167.

Esther. In a long article following the suggestions of von Rad in *Joseph,* S. Talmon, "'wisdom' in the Book of Esther," VT, Vol. XIII (1963), pp. 419–455, has urged extensive wisdom motifs in Esther.

This bibliography of course does not exhaust the titles which might be mentioned. Other summaries and critical bibliographical reviews include Roland Murphy, "Assumptions and Problems in Old Testament Wisdom Research," CBQ, Vol. XXIX (1967), pp. 407–418; E. Gerstenberger, "Zur altestamentlichen Weisheit," *Verkündigung und Forschung* (München: C. Kaiser, 1969); and R.B.Y. Scott, "The Study of the Wisdom Literature," *Interpretation,* Vol. XXIV (1970), pp. 20–45. Scott notes the older summaries which are still useful.

In American scholarship the contributions of Roland Murphy are of singular value in their capacity to discern the central issues and to provide balanced judgments. In addition to "Assumptions and Problems in Old Testament Wisdom Research" and "A Consideration of the Classification, 'Wisdom Psalms'" his articles include: "The Interpretation of Old Testament Wisdom Literature," *Interpretation,* Vol. XXIII (1969), pp. 289–301; "Form Criticism and Wisdom Literature," CBQ, Vol. XXXI (1969), pp. 475–483, *Introduction to the Wisdom Literature of the Old Testament* (Collegeville, Minn.: Liturgical Press, 1965); and "The Kerygma of Proverbs," *Interpretation,* Vol. XX (1966), pp. 3–14.

Finally, in the category which most concerns the present discussion we may note efforts at understanding the theological intention of wisdom teaching: W. Brueggemann, "Scripture and an Ecumenical Life-Style," *Interpretation,* Vol. XXIV (1970), pp. 3–19, and "The Triumphalist Tendency in Exegetical History," JAAR, Vol. XXXVIII (1970), pp. 367–380; B. Gemser, "The Spiritual Structure of Biblical Aphoristic Wisdom," *Adhuc Loquitur,* ed. A. van Selms and A. S. van Woude (Leiden: Brill, 1968), pp. 138–149; John F.

Priest, "Humanism, Skepticism, and Pessimism in Israel," JAAR, Vol. XXXIV (1968), pp. 311–326; and H. D. Preuss, "Erwägungen zum theologischen Ort alttestamentlicher Weisheit Literatur," EvTh, 30 (1970), pp. 393–417.

[handwritten margin note: Vol. 36]

Index of Scriptural References

Index of Authors

Topical Index